An Earthbound Angel

A Spiritual Awakening

An Earthbound Angel

A Spiritual Awakening

GRAHAM MACLAUREN

Text Graham MacLauren
Copyright © Graham MacLauren

First print November 2023

CONTENTS

PREFACE	9
1. THE START OF THE BEGINNING	11
2. EARLY TEENAGE YEARS – PART 1	23
3. EARLY TEENAGE YEARS – PART 2	37
4. MY SECOND BRUSH WITH DEATH	47
5. THE WORLD OF WORK AND GROWING UP	53
6. MY OWN PLACE IN THE WORLD	55
7. BECOMING THE BEST	65
8. TOASTMASTER TO THE QUEEN	73
9. TRAGEDY STRIKES	81
10. MY INTUITION RETURNS	89
11. THE END OF THE BEGINNING	93
12. MY CALLING TO WORK IN SPIRIT	107

13. REFLECTIONS ON MY LIFE 115

PREFACE

This book is dedicated to my brother Garry. Without him fully opening the door to the wonderful ability that I now possess, I doubt it would ever have happened.

My life only began to change after he passed away, and I will always be indebted to him for giving me opportunities that otherwise would never have been open to me. I am grateful, in particular, for the opportunities I now have to travel the world and to use my ability to heal hearts and minds and unite families who might be grieving.

This book will be the story of a journey, about how life changes as ability develops, and the way your whole being is questioned as you return to the way you were created, fifty per cent male and fifty per cent female. This can be very traumatic. Through this book, I hope to help people understand the journey and that when you are called, the signs are everywhere. You just have to recognise them.

It is my intention to commit the rest of my life to working for the spirit world in every way that I can. I am honoured, and I am proud to have been chosen to work for them.

1. THE START OF THE BEGINNING

It was my last chance. If I failed this time, I would not go on. I had tried so hard to open myself to Spirit for so long and received only silence in return. Everyone else in my group was developing, and Spirit was answering their calls. But for me, there was nothing. I knew those who had passed over were waiting, desperate to give me their messages of love and comfort, but I could not break through the barrier in my mind and let them in.

I sat in a circle every week with my colleagues in the group and only missed two sessions in 18 months because I committed myself to it. In the first twelve months, I got nothing. When Margaret, the tutor, asked me what came up in the meditation, all I said was, 'Cool, sorted.' But eventually, she wouldn't accept that anymore. I laughed because the group told newcomers to keep it short and sweet, but I was getting nothing at all. Was it a trust issue, or did I not have the comprehension or belief that I had this ability? I just didn't believe that I could talk to spirit.

My tutor initially wanted me to be a speaker, not a medium. I had been asked if I wanted to attend this workshop being run by a visiting medium from Blackburn. Her name was Val, and she was an accomplished medium and well-respected minister, but on arrival, I realised I was the only male there, which was very intimidating. I wondered what on earth I was doing. Val spotted this instantly, and before I could make my excuses and leave, she got me working with a girl I knew from my group. Each time the pairs took turns, Val would ask if anyone in the group understood the message that had been received.

In the workshop, I listened while my friend gave her message. She said it was from my maternal grandmother, and she said it was the words Star and Phenomenal. I laughed this off and thanked her. And then the instructor looked at me. In a second exercise, Val asked another friend and I to connect and give our messages aloud. As the first of us gave their messages, with dread in my stomach, I was thinking, 'I can't do this!' and then I heard Val's voice as she said:

'It's your turn, Sunbeam!'

What's the point? I thought. But she had faith in me, so I had to try.

The familiar feeling crept over me, and I knew Spirit was near. I closed my eyes.

And suddenly, there it was, like a white light inside my head. 'I have a woman – the letter D – Diane or Diana – two children – blonde hair! She moved up a social class when she married. There's something about a phone call – and Paris – and danger.' I paused. *What had happened to her?* Then it came to me. 'She died of a broken heart!'

I opened my eyes and looked at everyone. They were all staring at me, and my instructor had gone pale.

'My God,' she said. 'I believe who you have with you is Diana, Princess of Wales!'

AN EARTHBOUND ANGEL

I was elated. The Princess, whom I had met on several occasions, had chosen to come to me! I knew that from then on, my life would never be the same again. I had been lost for so many years, but now I had found the vocation that would give my life meaning and purpose, something I had been searching for from almost the moment I was born.

Because I was never meant to survive.

My first day on earth should have been my last. When I was born, the umbilical cord was wrapped so many times around my neck that I should have died. Doctors described this as a 'blue baby.' I would have died if it wasn't for the skill of the doctor who saved my life. Even then, he told my parents I likely wouldn't survive the night.

Against all odds, I did, and my grateful parents named me after him. But ever since that first day, I have never felt completely alone. I was an angel trapped on earth, and death would cast a shadow over me my entire life.

My parents got married when they were very young. My mother was 19 when she had me, and they had only been married for a year. But that is no excuse for how difficult they made my life. They say that we choose our parents before we are born. If I had known what my family life was to be like, I might have chosen differently.

I had very bad asthma for the first seven years of my life. I was a very sickly and nervous child, and I was afraid of everything. Even the family budgie terrified me!

No matter where we went, I always clung to my mother. That was a big problem for my parents because I wouldn't stay overnight anywhere except at my grandparents'. Even now, as an adult, I don't like staying away from home. I've got to get back to my safe place if I can.

So, if we were visiting anywhere, even family, we had to always come home. It must have been very frustrating for my mother, especially when my brother Garry was born just over a year after she had me.

Our house was very busy. My auntie and her kids stayed with us for a time. My father was in the Territorial Army, and he was a drinker, and he was always bringing people home. We would never know who was coming and going. And there were a lot of parties. My brother and I were always sent to our room ('out of sight, out of mind'). When he was a bit older, Garry would sneak into the living room, go around all the unattended beer cans, and drink the dregs. We would spend ages looking for him, and then we would find him drunk behind the sofa.

My father was a real 'wheeler dealer' and would do whatever it took to make some cash. If something 'fell off the back of a lorry', you knew he was involved. But mostly, he worked as a lorry driver and an accomplished vehicle mechanic, and that could take him away from home for days at a time. We were so used to him being away that when he was sent to prison for driving offences, we believed my mother when she told us he was just working.

She might have been grateful for the break because he also had a temper. He believed he was the master of the house and his word was law. He would stay out drinking all night and come home with some distressed woman we had never met before. Then he would order my mother out of bed to entertain them. If she refused, he would beat her until she did. I would cower away, trying to make myself small so I wouldn't catch his attention, covering my ears to shut out his raised voice and the sounds my mother made when he hit her. Those are memories that will never leave me.

For a child, it was horrific. I think that's where my desire for escapism came from. From an early age, I knew this world just wasn't for me. I was a kind child, and animals and little children loved me. I remember my mum telling me about the first time she had brought me home from the hospital and how she had laid me on the chest of the family dog, a boxer called Candy. And the dog just folded her paws over me to stop me from falling, which was beautiful.

When I was older, and people with babies came to visit, I would be put in charge of the little ones because I could always get them off to sleep. Always. I would hold them or sway them in their cots, and they would stop crying and sleep.

That earned me no favours with my father, though. He used to beat me because I was too compassionate. 'There's no fight in you!' he would say as he brought his fists down again and again, and I would wonder what I had done to deserve such a life.

Garry was my Dad's favourite. He knew it, even when he went missing and was found playing with the coal man or the Midden Men (the bin men), and he'd be black with dirt, but he was still my father's favourite. For me, the belt or the fists would come down on me again and again.

We lived on the upper floor of a traditional block of four flats on Halbeath Avenue in Drumchapel, which was a very rundown part of Glasgow. We used to joke it was the posh part of Drumchapel because we had a veranda.

We knew all the neighbours and got on well with everyone but Mrs Creeney. She didn't like kids much and was forever knocking at our door, complaining about my brothers and I running up and down the hall playing. She lived below us, but her two boys often let Garry and I play pool or darts with them, especially her oldest son Dougie. He was cool, although we didn't see much of him because he was older and already working while we were still kids in school.

To keep out of the way, I used to play out on the landing. I had a magnetic blackboard on one side and chalk on the other, and I used to boss everybody around as if I were a teacher because that's what I wanted to be when I grew up. If I couldn't be a teacher, then I wanted to be a policeman so I could arrest my father for everything he had done to my mother.

I went to nursery when I was three or four, but my first memories are of school. I really didn't enjoy it. The trauma in my home life overshadowed everything else. I just didn't want to be on Earth and didn't know how to tell anybody. It was as if there was a barrier between me and the rest of the world that I didn't know how to get through. I also missed a lot of school, as I suffered from asthma and had to attend regular appointments at Yorkhill Hospital.

But children will find joy even when their lives are hard. I remember going to the Argos Centre on a Saturday, which was the youth centre near the school. We used to go there to play indoor football and snooker and cards and things like that. It was supervised, and there were lots of games organised for us. Sometimes we'd follow the flute and accordion bands as they passed by, not understanding why they played louder outside the chapel than they'd done along the roads. I'd be watching out for my uncle in the accordion band, who was good with it too. My best friend David lived in the close next door, but although we were the same age, he went to the Catholic School, and I attended the Protestant one. It was the same with Sunday School - I went to the church, but he went to the chapel. Only at the Argos Centre could we play together without religion being a problem.

One of my favourite memories comes from when I was about five years old, around the time my second brother, Colin, was born. Princess Margaret, the sister of the late Queen, was coming to open the shopping centre close to where we lived. I had gone along to see her (with my class from school), and my grandmother came there to see me. I always had to have the latest gadgets, so my grandmother bought me a set of 'Pop-a-Point' pencils. I was very proud of them; they were all I could think about. So, when Princess Margaret came along, all I wanted was to show her my 'Pop-a-Point' pencils! And she stopped and looked at them and spoke to me for a few minutes until she moved on. It was my first brush with royalty! In the years to come, as I served her family, I would wonder if she remembered the little boy and his special pencils!

Despite these moments of happiness, I still wished I could find a way out of my life. And fate had been listening because when I was six, our downstairs neighbour, Mrs Creeney, found me lying unconscious on the concrete floor of the close.

It was a cold Winter's day, and I was playing out on the landing after school when I had the accident. Mrs Creeney couldn't wake me, and there was fluid draining out of my right ear. She screamed for my parents, and I was rushed to hospital. I had fallen or been pushed from the upstairs landing, and my skull was fractured. Later, the doctors told us that I would have died if I hadn't been wearing my duffle coat with the hood up.

I was in the hospital for some time and remember it vividly. Parents were not allowed to stay with children in those days, and the staff were quite strict. Like most kids, I had a very sweet tooth, and my family brought me treats. But the nursing staff used to take all the sweets and share them with the other kids.

One day, my uncle and aunt came to see me, and they brought me a massive pink sugar mouse! Of course, I hid my sugar mouse under my pillow. And I would bite off wee bits of it every night when no one was looking. It was heaven! Eventually, I got caught, but they could do nothing because it was one big piece of sugar, and they couldn't share it!

My skull eventually mended, and I was allowed home, but that accident left me with a legacy. I have never recovered the hearing in my right ear.

AN EARTHBOUND ANGEL

The feeling that I was being watched and followed around became even more obvious as I got older. It terrified me and made me very insecure. In fact, I could not sleep in the dark. I had to have the door open or someone beside me until I was asleep because I was terrified that ghosts or vampires were going to get me. If only I'd known they were the spirit world trying to take care and protect me, it would have been a different story.

To make a little bit of money for myself and David, I started helping the paperboy with his deliveries. His name was Robert, and he used to pay me to help him. I think we got about fifty pence a week! We'd meet at the car park to collect the papers, but the older boys would bully David and I, and try to get us fighting over religion to see who'd crack first. It was never me; so many times, I got beaten up. Eventually, I hit David back, and he never again picked on me as we delivered the newspapers with Robert.

We would split the paper round between us, and eventually, we would get to the part that I dreaded. The chapel. I would take the papers from Robert and start walking up the driveway, dragging my feet as I went.

I was a big fan of the horror films made by Hammer Movies, especially the vampire ones. So, when I started seeing people come out of the headstones in the cemetery, all I could think was, *The vampires are coming for me!*

I had no idea that I was sensitive to Spirit, and they were, in fact, being drawn to me.

Then the priest would open the door, dressed all in black. By then, I was so scared I would throw his papers at him and run like the wind down the driveway in case something grabbed me and dragged me back! If only I had known that they meant me no harm!

Later, as I went up and down the closes that were six or eight in a stair, I could sense somebody following me. It was the same every time, but no matter how many times I turned around, nobody was there. I was always frightened, but I couldn't show that to Robert because, if he knew, he wouldn't let me deliver the papers with him, and I wouldn't get my money.

I even had the idea that I'd put an onion in my pocket (thinking that it was the same as garlic) and I'd carry a small stick to use as a stake, planning to make the cross sign with my fingers to keep me safe, especially at the chapel.

But there were worse things than ghosts to be afraid of, and I found out at a very young age that the worst monsters come in disguise.

At that time, my mother worked for the Scottish Opera, and we'd go to all the Highland Games at the weekends around the country. We'd meet the celebrities and badger Mum into letting us sell lottery tickets with her, hoping we'd sell a winner. Eventually, we had a stall where my Dad would set up a game called Chase the Ace. If someone poked the Ace out of the board, they would win £250. But strangely, no one would ever win, except my Dad, because he'd stripped the game down and rigged it. All the high-paying cards would get removed, meaning the house was always the winner. I think this game allowed us to go on holiday to Butlins in Skegness.

AN EARTHBOUND ANGEL

This continued for years until Mum decided to sell insurance instead. Around the same time, my aunt and uncle had gone to Australia with a view to immigrating there. My Dad hoped it would work out, and then he planned to fly out and join them with us soon after. But Australia didn't work out, and then my dad and uncle went to South Africa but returned after six months, saying that the apartheid system made it difficult to live and work.

With my mother's work, she was often out at night, and, of course, my father was never home, so my brothers and I were left with babysitters. Sometimes it would be Michelle, who lived in our block. She looked after us once a week, and I wished it could have been her every day. Because when she was unavailable, we were looked after by the boy who lived downstairs from us.

He was about ten years older than me, so he was supposed to be trustworthy. In his house, he had a pool table and a dartboard; during the day, he would sometimes invite us in to play darts with him and his brother. That was okay, and we got to know him, so my mother had no qualms about leaving him in charge. If only she had known.

I came to dread those nights.

It started when I was almost seven. He would bring his friend along with him to babysit, and, at first, everything would be normal. We would play for a while, and I would join in, trying to act as if nothing was wrong. But as the hours ticked by towards bedtime, trepidation would creep over me and build up until there was nothing inside me but dread. On the outside, I would be fine, playing a game with my brothers, but as it got later, I would see the sly glances between the older boys, and my heart would beat faster because I knew what they were planning.

And then it would be time for bed.

I would lie in the dark, praying for something to happen to save me. Maybe my mother would come home early. Maybe there would be an emergency downstairs. Maybe I could just close my eyes and never wake up. But that prayer was never answered. As soon as my brothers were safely asleep, the two boys would get me alone in my room. And what they did to me was something no child should ever have to suffer.

It was harrowing. When it was done, I would pray they would leave me alone. But they came back, over and over again, several times a night. When they were finally done, they threatened me with hell on earth if I told anyone. Only I knew that I was already there.

The abuse continued until we moved away three years later. But it would be years and years before I could face what happened and finally bring it to light.

2. EARLY TEENAGE YEARS – PART 1

I was lucky enough to know all my grandparents, but I was closest to my father's mother, who lived in Abbottshall Avenue — my gran, grandad and uncle. My gran used to tell us stories about my dad and his brother, and their friends Tommy and Danny, who wanted a rabbit but whose parents wouldn't allow it. My gran said they could keep a rabbit on her veranda, but they were just kids and didn't clean the rabbit cage. So she said they should give the rabbit away to the poor family down the road. Tommy and Danny cried afterwards, so my gran said; 'Maybe you should ask for the rabbit back?' But when they did, the poor woman gave them a paw each, which made them cry all the way home! Granny wasn't popular for that life lesson, but she did allow them to keep white mice for a while until one ran up her trouser leg. She hit the roof and the mice had to go too.

Gran worked as an insurance collector for Wesleyan and General Insurance which meant visiting people's houses every evening to collect their monthly insurance monies. One night, Granny and my mum and other women had taken part in a Ouija board session, where the messages were astounding. Mum said that it predicted that she and Dad would split up and the house would be broken into by one of the neighbours.

We had a beautiful red setter called Prince, who was timid and frightened of his own shadow. If he got off his lead, he would bolt. It was just before Christmas, and Mum had bought all the presents, and I was looking forward to getting my first record player. Garry wanted a Tonka truck to destroy. One day when Mum collected us from school, we returned to find the house HAD been burgled, just as she'd been told. But not through the door; they'd got in through the kitchen ceiling! The dog was barking at the hole which had been cut out, and we knew he must have known the burglar because he'd been up on the table, and his paw prints were visible around the ceiling hole. Mum went downstairs to the neighbours, knowing she couldn't prove anything, but she sat with them while they had their tea and told them that she'd been burgled and what had been taken, including a couple of extra big ticket items. The neighbour's son began to disagree and then realised he'd confessed, so he told us that he and his pal had done it. We didn't get most of our stuff back, but I did eventually get a record player, which I treasured.

From an early age, my mother used to tell us that many people commended us on our good behaviour when we were out in public. My mother was a great baker, making amazing cakes and shortbread, but I remember she made caramel shortbread for my cousin, which made me think she loved him more than us. My cousins were better off and would tease us for not having a lot. My mum used to say that maybe I'd been born to the wrong sister because I have very expensive tastes, whereas my cousin does not.

I remember visiting my uncle, who was in the army. We visited him and his wife in Catterick, where they lived with a beautiful Old English sheepdog called Gilbert. Gilbert was generally okay if I rolled around on the floor with him, until the day he bit me. When I got back from being patched up at the hospital, he licked the side of my face and cuddled into me as if he knew he'd done something wrong. How intuitive animals are!

Gran and Grandad finally got a break and moved to Glendarule Avenue in the middle of Bearsden, which was a very posh area of Glasgow. Ellen McLaren (known as Nell) was a wee woman who packed a punch! As I grew older, she would become closer to me than my own mother. Later, she would even give up her home to be where I was. I think it was because she could see what was happening with me. She was always my protector. Always.

One day when we were visiting her house in Bearsden, my brother and I were out in her garden with her two King Charles spaniels, Candy and Mandy. It was a hot day, and we were very thirsty.

I shouted to my gran, 'Granny, gees a drink a' watter'!'

She put on her best posh voice and said, 'Speak properly, child!'

Garry and I looked at each other. What was that all about? There was nothing else for it. We put on our best posh voices and shouted, 'Granny gees a drink a' watter, *please!*'

I'll never forget the day we found out we were moving to Bearsden. My brother and I were in the back of the car, and it pulled up outside a house. When we saw that the 'For Sale' sign had been taken down, we realised we were moving. We turned to each other and shared the biggest hug ever.

I was 9, Garry was 8, and Colin was only 3 when we found out we were moving. We were no longer ruffians from the slums! I was finally going to escape from Drumchapel and everything that had happened to me there. The only downside was that the three of us would have to share as it was a two-bedroom house. But my Dad was very handy and we'd soon get extra space once we were settled. I could finally be free.

My mother's parents lived on the south side of Glasgow, at a place called Priesthill. We used to go there every Sunday for lunch or dinner, and we used to meet my Gran McDevitt on a Saturday in town to go shopping. We'd always meet at Henry Healy, the butchers in Glasgow, and then we'd traipse all over town. Then we'd go to the Alhambra for dinner, and we would get a treat. The highlight of the year was the pantomime. They took us every year, and that was great.

My Grandad McDevitt (Willie to his friends) was a terribly funny man. He worked in Weirs Pumps in Cathcart with my uncle. He'd even helped his son with his business in Kilmarnock carpet fitting. Grandad was a great artist, and he painted and fixed Airfix models with us. He'd bribe us to tickle his feet or rub his back, but he was much older than Gran McLaren and very frail. He liked to doodle, and he had a fascination for clocks. Grandad could take a watch to bits and put it back together again (unlike me), but I think I get my love of antique clocks from him. He was a great joker and good with the kids. He'd bounce them on his knee and sing crazy songs that ended with a 'YeeeHaaa!' to make us laugh and giggle.

He died when I was eight. He had smoked like a chimney all his life, and he died of lung cancer. It was a very sad loss.

It was my first funeral, and I was taken to the chapel for the Mass, where I clung to my mum throughout. I watched the hearse being walked away from the chapel, and we left to visit my auntie Mary and my cousins who lived up the road. My great-aunt Annie and Auntie Helen lived nearby, along with Auntie Bessy. Bessy and Helen lived in high-rise flats, and boy, was it tough when the lift was out of action! Great-Aunt Annie didn't have kids, and either hadn't married, or her husband has passed away by the time I was old enough to remember. She also loved to bake and would give us pocket money when we visited. My uncle and aunt lived across the playground from Annie, so when we visited, it was like visiting the Waltons on the South Side! Like Dallas but without the money!

My uncle Billy worked at Spillers dog food factory in Barrhead. After he separated from my auntie, he married another Mary and lived at Cardonald on the South side until he went to work in Asia. He began his own business and travelled the world as an engineer deploying specialised equipment, but he eventually returned with what we thought was influenza, but after he passed away in his 40s, we were told he was the first person to die of SARS.

He had lived near my gran and grandad before he moved to Cardonald. My grandparents continued to live on the same rundown street, and my gran lived in Househill, Muir Road in Priesthill in the same house all their days. It was a rough area at the time and there were lots of burglaries, but their house was never touched. Never. Gran had no choice but to move to Rutherglen for the last days of her life until she died in a diabetic coma.

Later in life, I learned that Grandad McDevitt's family were shoemakers from Edinburgh, but not just any shoemakers. They made shoes for the elite. They lived in a penthouse above what used to be the Littlewoods retail store on Frederick Street, so obviously, they were very well-to-do. My grandfather was disinherited, however, when he met my grandmother because she was a commoner. His family thought she was beneath him because she was in service.

They loved each other deeply, and this just goes to show that no matter where you are from, when love prevails, you can be happy with the right soul. My friends say it takes a long time to find the right person, but they are out there. Luckily my gran and grandad met early in life. A love story in itself.

Moving to Bearsden changed my life. I made new friends, Fiona and Ewan, whose dad was the janitor at the school. Ewan was the same age as me, so I used to kick about with him. We used to have parties in the house when his mum and dad were away for the weekend!

AN EARTHBOUND ANGEL

We were always busy. We used to put on shows in the old folk's home behind the school. I don't know what the old folks thought of them, but we had a great time!

We were lucky to have a playroom attached to our room in the attic of our house. We set up a CB radio to talk to our friends using outrageous handle names. I was 'Evil Genius', and my friend Tony was 'Tartan Bam.' One night, my parents were visiting our next-door neighbour who played at the Berkeley Club in Glasgow and went on to star as the Ice-Cream Man in the film 'Comfort and Joy.' Garry was on our CB radio, and I was watching him as the babysitter, being the oldest. The next thing, all we could hear, coming through the TV, was Garry swearing on the radio. My Dad went mental, and I got the blame as usual. Nothing much had changed even though we'd moved!

I went to Colquhoun Park Primary School, just two streets away. My teacher was Mrs O'Boyle, who was a tyrant. It was noticed that I had issues with my sight and needed glasses, but I hated them when the torture started in the playground. Most days, I'd go home, and the glasses were either broken or in my pocket. I hated them so much.

One of the greatest things that changed my life at that time was the Bearsden and Milngavie Corps of Drums. It was run by Arthur and Sarah, who ran the SPAR shop across the road from us. Every time I went to the shop, they talked to me about joining the band until I agreed.

I wasn't very musical, but I was the right height to hold the cymbals for the snare drummers. Some of my friends who lived in the same street were in the band too, and we used to take part in marching band competitions all over the country.

We used to perform at things like the opening of housing developments, and the highlight for me was the football at the weekend. Our uniforms were the colours of the Rangers Football strip. How excited this made me to go to the football at the weekends supporting the team in my kit. We used to play music at halftime, and we were allowed to sit and watch the match. We trained at Kilmardinny Playing Fields in the summer and Colquhoun Park in the winter, where we'd use the gym or dining hall on wet days. I hated having to polish the cymbals, but it was a sense of responsibility to clean and look after a valuable piece of kit, my uniform, and my Shako hat.

I also joined the Boys' Brigade. I was in Westerton, and I took it seriously. I was a short-distance runner for the Boys' Brigade and competed in 100 and 200-metre races.

I also did their Bible class competitions at the district level. For these competitions, I had to read lots of books. Then I had to answer questions on the books, followed by an inspirational reading about a person they nominated. For me, it was John Wesley, the Methodist reformer. I read so much about him that his life story became ingrained in my brain. I couldn't wrap a parcel with string, as they say, but I sure could talk about John Wesley! It was church every week, and when we were on parade for Remembrance Day, you felt amazing and so grown up, being with the Senior Section and the Officers. It was a great structure to instil in kids who didn't have any structure in the rest of their life.

I think that's partly where all my inspiration comes from now. That early training in public speaking from the Boys' Brigade has stood me in good stead over the years.

I was ten when I joined, so I was nearing the end of the junior section. Because I did so well with my running, I was asked if I would take over the 'Bulldog' group when the captain left. It was quite a responsibility. I had to make sure the younger kids in my care were clean, well presented and had their hats on properly. Shoes polished, clothes clean and pressed, nails and hands clean, hat straight and badges and armband straight. It really was all about discipline.

At the end of the year, there was a celebration that was something to do with the Wizard of Oz. We had to dress up as scarecrows! It was quite amazing.

Everyone was invited to watch us perform and afterwards see us collect our achievement awards. I got an award for running 'Bulldog', even though I'd only had the group for half the year, so I must have been good at it!

Miss Russell - she was an officer. She seemed like a dragon, but she nurtured you in her own way to get the best from you. And when she presented me with an award, she just smiled as if to say, 'Now you know why I was hard on you.' She was a pussycat in costume, I'm sure.

Before I knew it, I was ready for high school and Company Section at the Boys' Brigade. I was looking forward to it. My brothers were at Colquhoun Park, and I went to Boclair Academy in Bearsden. Boclair was the best school in the area, especially after Bearsden Academy had the scandal of an adult going back to school and pretending to be a kid. Later, I watched the TV about him, and I'm sure, I met him with my friends.

To get there, we had to take the bus. I became friendly with the bus driver, so I collected all the tickets for him and added up all the money. It was great! I felt very adult because I was taking the money and operating the machine. It was one of those old-fashioned machines with a handle that turned and spat out the ticket. Because I helped him out, I got to travel for free!

Things were looking up for all of us. When we moved to Bearsden, my father got a new job. He became a delivery driver for Walter Black, a company that made sauces and pickles and things like that. When Garry and I were off school, we used to go and help him with his deliveries.

Dad was never out of the garage, where there was always a car needing some small cash job that he was working on. He was a good mechanic, and regularly the garage floor had to be repainted to cover the oil stains. I used to go to Clydebank with my Gran on Sundays to work in the family shop. The entire family worked there at some point, it seemed, and this shop was everything. It was a cafe, a deli, a corner shop, a driving school and a clothes shop, all at once. It was just under the railway bridge in Clydebank on Station Road, opposite the station Bar. Gran and I used to eat all the chocolate snowballs on a Sunday and we loved it. Mum used to send Garry and I to Snips at the end of the road for our haircuts, and we were always told to get a 'short back and sides', never anything else. Even though, boy, we tried. Bearsden was the happiest time of my life.

It was a happy time, but, of course, it was not to last. My life was about to change once more, and not for the better.

It was a Sunday night when I was about twelve. At that time my mother worked for Refuge Insurance, and she had been down south at a conference. On the way back, she was in a serious car accident, just like the accident she'd had years before (when a deaf driver ran a red light and bounced the car across the road, bouncing off the barriers underneath the Kingston Bridge.) Someone rammed into the passenger side of her car. The car was badly damaged, and she could have been killed, but somehow, she managed to drive it home. Garry and I said that the car was specially made for going around corners because of the massive dent in the middle of the two doors!

I don't know exactly what happened, but she ended up in a big argument with my father. Then she just walked out. Their relationship had been volatile for years; perhaps she had finally had enough. My belief is both my mother and father were having affairs, even though she denied it.

All I knew is that something was slammed on the glass table, and it shattered, right before my mother walked out the door. She took nothing and left without even a word to her children. She just left us behind.

A school dance was coming up, and I remember my home economics teacher Mrs Ainslie asked me if I was going to the dance. I said no. She asked me why not, and I told her that my parents had separated, and we couldn't afford the ticket. She just opened her arms and held me.

AN EARTHBOUND ANGEL

When I looked up, she was in tears, and she said, 'I'll pay for your ticket.'

It was so touching of her. Mrs Ainslie was just a wee woman in her sixties, but she had such compassion. She was in tears, saying to me, 'Now, you'll definitely come. Or will I have to come and pick you up?' I couldn't have that. So I said, 'Yes, I'll go,' which I did, but my heart was broken thinking my whole family was in pieces now. Gran came down to help with meals and keeping the house in between her work at the garage. Gran and my aunt worked in the local petrol station where they lived, and it ran like clockwork between them. Gran would get brought down to us, and she'd get us organised, too, before she'd leave or stay over, depending on what we needed.

My mother used to call us to make sure we were all right. For weeks after she left, my father beat me to make sure I was crying when she phoned to get her to come back.

He would say, 'There's the phone; speak to your mother.'

I would speak to her, in tears, in the hope that she would come back. Because it was me she had left behind. But she never did.

Very shortly after they separated, my father moved his new woman and her two children into the house, and I couldn't cope. I had a nervous breakdown. I don't think my father realised what it would do to me at this stage of my life. No one noticed I was broken.

AN EARTHBOUND ANGEL

It was even worse when we visited my stepmother's mother, who was an alcoholic. She got worse when she lost her partner, and if you went into the living room, you'd need a helmet as whisky bottles got thrown at you, but often missed as the marks on the door showed. She was probably still grieving, but when she was sober, she could be funny. Her false teeth never fitted properly, and this affected her speech, but I often used to give her a cuddle, and I prayed she got peace in her life because I thought she wouldn't last much longer if she carried on this route. Sadly she passed away in her sixties.

My young life had been a rollercoaster. I had gone from the fear of nearly dying to the fear of being abused continually to what I thought was a settled period. Now I felt so bad I could have just walked down the main road and let the traffic hit me. I wanted the pain to be over. I wanted to die.

It is a feeling that has never left me. It has always been in the background, even when times have been good. Now I am an adult, it is still the same. I wouldn't take that final step; I'm not stupid. I don't have that kind of courage anyway, but if a door appeared and someone said, 'Come through this door and never come back to this life again,' I would go through it in a heartbeat.

I don't have any pictures of my childhood or my family. My father and my mother must have destroyed them all. When my mother walked out, she had no need for those memories.

She left them, and us, behind.

Given that we had a settled life, I couldn't understand why two people would need to have someone else. I had the feeling that both my mother and father had affairs and had partners waiting in the wings. But what about us? The kids? I certainly wasn't wanted, and all I could think about was going home to a place where I'd be loved. Something like getting back to the spirit. Even when my uncle and aunt were going on holiday, they took my younger brother Garry, not me. This was a big turning point in how Garry treated me and my uncle and aunt too. Again, my feelings of loss and sadness were back, and the only people I could talk to were those in my head.

And they couldn't help set me free.

3. EARLY TEENAGE YEARS – PART 2

I couldn't cope with my stepmother and her kids. My father moved her in too quickly. I hadn't met this woman or got to know her. She just arrived and that was it. She was to be our Mum.

I wanted out of there. I wanted to stay with my real mum. Eventually, she agreed I could, and she took me to my gran's house at Priesthill. I loved it there, but soon I was on the move again. My mother took me to my aunt's house in Rutherglen, where I was to go to school.

I hated it there because I had nowhere to call my own. I had to sleep on the floor in my cousin's bedroom because, even though there was a spare room, they used it as a TV lounge and refused to turn it into a bedroom for me.

When I was in Rutherglen, my Grandad McLaren died. My gran had a terrible life with him. He was very like my father. He used to hit my gran, but he was faithful to her. He worked for the electricity board, and he was only 57 when he died.

I loved that man. And now he was gone. I'm sure he loved my Gran, and he was only trying to be protective of her, especially after she got mugged when out collecting insurance money. After her mugging, my grandad ran my gran around in the car to cover her route. She was badly shaken. And I didn't know how she would cope now that Grandad had passed. She'd have to sell her house in Spain. And it was just as well that she lived with my uncle and aunt in Bearsden. So she wasn't on her own. I always said to Gran, 'I'll come and live with you when I'm old enough.' But, of course, that never happened.

After she sold the houses in Spain, she allocated money to all the grandchildren and took us on a spending spree. As I was the oldest, she'd told me about this special store in Glasgow where personal service was key. As we walked the streets of Glasgow, Gran had thousands of pounds in her carrier bag. She told me no one would think to steal from her. She was sharp and witty and never missed a beat. Once, as a teenager, she told me about a gent's store where I could get fitted for a suit and where my uncle, father and others bought their suits. She said that when we went in, they would take my jacket and ask what side I dressed on before measuring me. I cringed to discuss such things with my Gran and wished the ground would open and swallow me up. But I replied that I understood, and she just smiled, and it was okay.

My gran phoned to ask my mum to take me to the funeral. I will never forget that day. It was a cremation, and I was totally unprepared for what happened — the curtain opening and sliding away to reveal the plinth with the coffin disappearing down the centre as you watched it before the automated curtain met in the middle again. It was like a coffin on a table runner. My aunt nearly passed out. It was one of the worst things I had ever seen in my short life.

When we came outside, my grandmother was in the back of the undertaker's black limousine, and she was in a state. She was wearing a fur coat, and I'll never forget how she put her arms around me and didn't want to let me go. She opened her purse and poured everything into my hands, telling me how much she and my grandad loved me.

I had started at Stone Law High School. The teachers would ask if I was some kind of school inspector or if I tried out schools for councils as I looked older. It was awful. I hated it. What I witnessed in the classroom were pregnant teachers being a target with kids throwing tennis balls to see who could hit the bump. It was just fearful. No wonder that no teaching happened there. I was the new boy who got spat on from behind and had chewed paper thrown at him. It was all getting too much for me. I used to have memories from my younger days when my mum took us to visit her sister in John Menzies in Rutherglen, and they'd tell me to shut my eyes and think that I was going to be getting sweets, and then it was so. My mother could show off my long eyelashes to my aunt's work colleagues, but this became torture itself after school. I tried so hard not to go home thinking about how to escape this hell. I'd think about all the things I could do to die and never come back, but I tried to put a good face on it and say, 'Yes sir, no sir, 3 bags full, sir.' But no one could see how I was hurting inside except those voices in my head. Now Grandad was there too. Could he help? 'Please?' I begged him. Could he help? When I got home, I'd have to do my paper run. My cousin used to do it, but he was older now, and his sister and I got to do it instead. My mother was still baking, and my cousin was getting treated better than I was. I would have been better off in a children's home. Life couldn't get any worse.

Or could it?

My mother only saw me at weekends. So what was a family or love? I joined the senior section of the Boys Brigade at the 5th Rutherglen on Stonelaw Road. My uncle was an officer, and I'd get the chance to develop some of my skills, or so I thought, but it wasn't to be, and I didn't really enjoy it there. Although I met Drew, and he made life bearable, my cousin continued bullying me. And made my school life hell, being only a year or two older than me.

I suffered at Rutherglen for about six months before my mum got a house at Cathkin. It was a relief to be there, just the two of us. I had my own room again! However, we were only there a few months when she decided without discussion that we were moving in with her boyfriend, Pat, and his family, who lived at Shawhead, the worst part of Coatbridge you could ever imagine.

I was only 14, and I was on the move again. That meant another new school, which turned out to be a very rough one, and I got bullied mercilessly because I was considered a 'posh boy'. They called me every name under the sun. They threw things at me and stole my stuff. It was a very, very hard time.

I hated Pat, and my stepbrother was horrible to me. I got the blame for everything. No matter what happened, he ran to Daddy, and I got the blame. Pat's son Charles lived at home for a while, and he and I got on, but soon he moved out.

Back to the torture of the daily grind, trying to work out how to get out of this hell that was my life. Why didn't my Grandad's help, or perhaps they tried? My head was bursting, and all I wanted and needed was love, just like Gran gave me.

I just didn't want to be there. If it was a rollercoaster that I was riding, I soon realised there were no ups. The trajectory was purely downwards: from Bearsden to Priesthill to Rutherglen to Coatbridge. I had gone from a very respectable area where I could have made something of my life to the slums and from being loved to being ignored, or worse. What had I done to deserve this?

I had my own room in Coatbridge, but I never had any peace. My stepbrother made my life hell. Eventually, I couldn't take it anymore. I decided to run away.

My gran, my uncle and my aunt had moved to Rose Cottage in Killermont. I decided that was where I would go, but I made the mistake of telling a friend I was running away to be with my gran.

I managed to sneak out of the house, and I phoned her from a public call box to tell her I was coming. My uncle told me where to get a taxi and said they would pay for it. I remember getting in the car and telling the driver I was going to Rose Cottage, Killermont, Bearsden. It was such a relief.

They made me welcome and made a big fuss of me. I went to bed content for the first time in what felt like forever. I had no intention of going back. I'd had enough of it. I didn't have a life there.

Later that night, there was a knock on the door. It was the police. They had come to take me back.

My wishes didn't matter. I had to go. I tried to resist. I clung onto my gran and, until the day she died, she had scars on her arm from my nails as they dragged me away.

When I got back to Coatbridge, I told my mother I wasn't staying. I said I wanted to see my brothers. They had stayed with my father, and I hadn't seen them for two years. There was some discussion, but in the end, I got my way. It was agreed I would leave the following day. It seemed like a victory. I might not have been so sure if I had known what awaited me.

The house in Bearsden had been sold, and my father had left Glasgow. He was now living in a caravan with my brothers, my stepmother, and her son at Seton Sands Holiday Village on the east coast. My gran had a holiday home there, so it kind of made sense. One of my stepmother's sons must have had similar thoughts because he went to live with his father, who'd immigrated to Australia.

I was hoping for a new start, but my heart sank as soon as I got there. The caravan had only two bedrooms, so four of us had to share one room. It was vile.

I had gone from what I thought was the slums to an even more cramped slum. Still, I hoped the trauma would be over and things would improve, but it was not to be. I was there on sufferance. I learned to keep my head down because if I misbehaved at all, it was, 'Pack your bags, you're leaving.'

And my father beat the hell out of me until I gave up all contact with my mother.

Surely, I could go no lower? Then my step mum had a baby boy, so we had Garry, Colin, Scott and myself, and we now also had a baby to squeeze into the two-room caravan.

I was enrolled in Preston Lodge High School in Prestonpans. It was my fourth high school, and I started there in my third year. I hated it. It was the worst school I had attended. The teachers ignored me and left me to my own devices.

When I was 15, my gran moved to Port Seton. I knew she didn't trust my stepmother with the family, so she bought a residential unit to be near us. It was a big change for her. She had already had a holiday home there, but visiting in the summer was very different to living there all year round. She made that sacrifice for us.

It was thanks to her that I started earning some real money. Although I worked in the chip shop at the weekends, she helped me set up a private paper round. Every morning before school, I would ride my bike to the village, collect the papers and deliver them to the residents in the caravan park.

My gran and her friend Big Maggie worked and managed the site laundrette, so after school, I would collect and deliver laundry, and I got paid for that, too. Then I learned how to clean caravans. I was making a fortune!

The reality was I kept myself busy to escape the bad things in my life. I didn't want to be at home, and school was just horrible. I didn't get any qualifications, and I wanted to leave as soon as possible. I was supposed to stay on until the

Christmas after I was sixteen, but in August, when the new term started, I had no intention of going back.

Instead, my father arranged for me to go and work with him on work experience in the hope that they would take me on permanently. It was called a youth training scheme. He worked for a company in Dunbar that my uncle was affiliated with. It was called PCT Black Hawk and was a supplier to the Torness nuclear power station.

My father worked with a guy called Andy, who was a salesman, and he was amazing. He was a very old-fashioned gentleman.

As I got a little older, I found there were some advantages to living at Port Seton. It was a holiday town, so there were clubs and amusement arcades and bands. And girls! A different one every week.

My brother Garry and I used to pretend we were a lot older so we could get into the clubs all summer. My younger brother was phenomenal on the fruit machines and used to win a lot! And because we used to go and watch all the bands, I used to hang out with the DJs, who were all much older than me. Even though I was only sixteen, they used to take me out with them. And we'd be in all the pubs beforehand.

I'll never forget one night in the Wemyss bar in Port Seton. I was at the bar, ordering the vodkas. I turned and realised the man beside me was my father. I could tell right away he was drunk. He looked straight at me, and I thought he was going to go nuts, but all he said was, 'I'll have a pint.'

He beat me for it the following day, though.

AN EARTHBOUND ANGEL

4. MY SECOND BRUSH WITH DEATH

My father was a drinker, but that didn't usually stop him from driving, whether he was over the limit or not. Every Friday after work, we went to the pub with Andy. They had a few beers, and I had a cola. We ate some toasties, and then we went home.

One time I went on holiday with my grandmother and brother to her favourite place, Benidorm, to the Rio Park Hotel. I don't think there was a single day when Garry and I didn't drink beer. We spent Christmas and New Year in Spain and returned home, where I returned to working with my father.

On January 31, 1985, we went to the pub as usual, but for some reason,, my dad didn't drink that night.

We said goodnight to Andy and set out for home along the A1. It was around five o'clock in the evening, and it was already dark. My dad was driving, and I was in the passenger seat. We were in a brand-new Peugeot van that had only done about fifty miles. It should have been a normal journey home, and I was already looking forward to the weekend.

The road was busy at that time of night, and the rain was getting heavier and heavier so that you could hardly see in front of you.

I have no idea what happened, as all I can remember is there was an impact, and my life spiralled as the car spun.

When it stilled, my dad asked if I was okay, but I told him I couldn't feel my legs. As my dad got out, he saw it was a JCB mechanical digger he'd hit. Our little vehicle had no chance. We'd smashed right into the digger.

The digger driver offered to pull the front of the car away to get me out, but he would have taken my legs with him if he had.

The accident was on the six o'clock news. It was a five-car pile-up, and the A1 was closed for hours. I was trapped in the van. I couldn't feel my legs. I was scared. I was cold. The engine was pressing into me. The roof was far too close. I really thought that my life was over.

It took three and a half hours to cut me out. If the van had been an older vehicle, I would have died at the scene. I remember the paramedics saying, 'Talk to us, Graham. Graham, talk to us. Don't shut your eyes.'

My spirit was leaving my body. I could feel myself transcending. Then there was water all over me, and I was shocked back into my body.

I remember them saying they were going to lift me out. Then I remember nothing until they were cutting off my clothes in the Royal Infirmary in Edinburgh.

As I lay there, pain in every nerve of my body, the hospital disappeared around me. Suddenly I was running through a field towards a ranch-style house with my uncle's dog beside me. There were lots of people at the house calling out to me and I was running towards them with the dog, feeling no pain whatsoever.

Suddenly, as I got near the house and everybody in it, I was grabbed by the scruff of the neck and pulled backwards at breakneck speed through a massive white light.

I heard the surgeon Mr Christie say, 'The time of death is…' and then my heart started to beat again. The next thing I remember is waking up in a world of pain, with weights pulling on my legs to straighten them and metal all around me.

I was the only person in that five-car pile-up who was seriously injured. The rest got away with minor scratches.

My mother's cousin phoned my mother to tell her, and I believe my mother was offered a police escort to the hospital. She didn't take it. She never came to see me at all. Years later, when I asked her why, she told me, 'Your father wouldn't let me see you.' I didn't believe her.

I ended up in Ward Five of the Royal Infirmary. It was an adult ward, and I was the youngest patient there. I was kept near the nurse's station because my condition wasn't great. At that point, they thought I would never walk again.

My worst injury was a serious compound fracture to the femur of my left leg. They used a Grosse and Kempf pin to repair my femur, and I was one of the first people in the world to undergo the procedure. It was a complicated process that needed three operations.

First, the damaged bone marrow was hollowed out, and the pin was inserted down the middle of the bone and pinned at the hip and the knee in the hope that healthy bone marrow would grow around the pin.

Then as the marrow grew, there was another operation to rotate the pin. Eventually, the bone marrow had grown enough that the pin could be taken out. That was the third operation. I did keep the pin for some time, but I don't know where it went to.

I was in the hospital for over eight months, so I got to know all the staff very well. Bridget used to do the night shift, and at four o'clock in the morning, she would make toast for us to share. On Fridays, we used to get a Chinese takeaway.

Any patients in for the long term were moved to the side ward, where there were only 6 beds, and they moved you along depending on how long you were there. There was a Norwegian guy opposite me who had been in a bike accident. He spoke no English, so, to pass the time, I taught him English and, in return, he taught me Norwegian. That was useful in later years when I did some work in Norway.

At long last, I was allowed to go home. Mima, who was a cleaner, organised a party for me the day before I was going home. We had sweets and cakes that she had baked, and all the nursing staff came in. It was amazing. They were in tears that I was finally going home, back to the caravan.

I was so frightened I could hardly bring myself to get in a car or van again. I had no other option in order to go home, but I couldn't bend my leg to get in the back, so I ended up in the middle seat, where I could pull the handbrake if I was frightened. I somehow felt reassured that there was someone with me again who would keep me from causing an accident.

Back at home, I got picked up by ambulance for my outpatient and physiotherapy appointments, but soon I was able to get around on crutches, and I could get the bus to my appointments.

The second time I got the bus, I bumped into a man who was getting on as I was getting off. He apologised, then looked at me more closely and said, 'Oh my God.'

I said, 'Sorry?'

And he said, 'Can you hold on a second?'

He went into his briefcase and took out the front page of *The Daily Record* newspaper. It was a story about me. His name was Ronnie, and he was the ambulance driver that had saved my life! In tears, he said, 'They told us you had died!'

But I had survived. Again.

5. THE WORLD OF WORK AND GROWING UP

Once I could walk again, I needed to find a job. I was friendly with a guy whose parents owned the café and the chippy on the high street, and he asked me if I wanted to come and work as a pizza chef. Now pizza had just hit the UK at this point, and it was very popular. I made up the pizzas for collection, and we were always busy. One night they were short of staff for the bar. It was another opportunity that I was keen to take, so I started learning how to work behind the bar.

From there, I got a job in the Caprice restaurant in Musselburgh. I was very successful there and was awarded 'Young Waiter of the Year' two years in a row.

My father and stepmother got a house in Port Seton, so we all moved there into a house with four bedrooms. No more living in the slums! Finally, it seemed my rollercoaster was on the way up again.

After the Caprice, I got a job at Pizzaland on Hanover Street in the centre of Edinburgh. There I met Alan and Scott. Alan was the manager, and Scott was his brother. They lived in Easter Road.

One night at work, the three of us came up with an idea. We decided we were going to buy a mobile disco, and that's what we did. We called it Midnight Express, and it was very successful. We worked it around our main jobs.

If we weren't working, we would go clubbing, and I would stay at Scott and Alan's on a Friday and Saturday night. We'd come in drunk and fall into bed, then the taxi would pick us up at eight o'clock on a Sunday morning to take us to work again.

Life was good, and it was about to get better. When I was 18, I met a girl called Lesley who worked in one of the shops near Pizzaland. She was training to be a nursery nurse. We went out together for a year, and we had a lot of fun, so naturally, we got engaged.

All this time, I was waiting for the insurance settlement from the accident. I discussed it a lot with my gran and Jack, her companion. We called Jack Noddy because he had a wee red car, rather large ears and a bald head. But Jack and I loved each other as if he were my grandfather or sent by him to look after my gran and me. He was the voice of reason for me, and when my father and I had a blowout, and he threw me out again, Jack would say, 'Come here, son,' and my gran would do her usual trick to smooth things over for me.

When the insurance settlement finally came, my stepmother and my father wanted me to spend it all on them.

My aunt said, 'No, that's not happening. It's his money.'

I knew what I was going to do with it. I was going to escape!

6. MY OWN PLACE IN THE WORLD

The money was my chance to finally escape my father's house. I found a flat that I liked and put in an offer. I could hardly believe it when it was accepted. Something good had finally happened!

I was keen to get it finalised, so I set up an appointment with the building society to sort out my mortgage. I was so naive I thought you took the actual money for the deposit, so I took the money out of the bank and hid it under the floorboards in my brother's house. When I came back for it, it was five thousand pounds short. Garry had stolen five thousand pounds and used the money to buy a car and some furniture for his house.

That was a problem. Now I didn't have enough money for the deposit. I wanted to phone the police, but my father wouldn't let me. He said he would disown me if I phoned the police. I had no idea what to do. I only knew it had to get sorted out. I wasn't going to lose this chance.

It was down to my gran in the end. The solution we finally agreed upon was to put Garry's name on the deeds for my flat. This meant that although Garry's name was on the deeds, he'd pay nothing towards my flat, but when I sold it, he'd get nothing from the sale either. I agreed this with my gran, and she sorted it out with my father and brother. It was hard because he'd stolen five thousand pounds from me, and it was clear that he was jealous of me too. But it would be my flat, and he would get no benefit from it whatsoever.

Now I was a homeowner at the tender age of 19! I could stay in my own flat on a Sunday night! No more trailing up and down to Port Seton.

Working at Pizzaland was great fun. I was awarded 'Employee of the Year' and won a voucher for a holiday. It was great working there, but I was always after more. I was part of the team that introduced the Seven Rules of Selling, which United Biscuits rolled out through all their units.

I left Pizzaland for a job in Café Plaza at Waverley Market, where I became the assistant manager.

All of this time, my mother played no part in my life. I hadn't seen her since I was 14, and she had not come to visit me when I was seriously injured. It took a bereavement to bring us together again.

Around January 6 that year, I got a phone call from my aunt, telling me that my Gran McDevitt had died and been cremated, all without my knowledge. That was devastating. While I was reeling from that news, she asked, 'Would you be prepared to meet your mum?'

I decided I would. It was so strange to see her after all that time, and I didn't know how to react at first, but gradually, we built a relationship again and became very close. Finally, there was some love in my life again. My father didn't like the idea of me giving my mother the car I had bought to drive once I passed my test. But it was just sitting there waiting for me to find the courage to learn how to drive, and my mother's car had been written off. She lived so rurally that I asked if she wanted it until I passed my test. I had no clue of how to learn to drive, but it wasn't going to be on the streets of Edinburgh, and I had the fear of the accident in the back of my mind, along with a push from somewhere to get it done. Someone in the spirit world was sending me signs which I ignored at the time.

When my mother came back into my life, she and Pat were married, and they had bought a house between Glasgow and Edinburgh. Because of my car accident, I was nervous about driving again, but my mother pushed me to overcome the fear. I was dropped at her house one day, and she said, 'We're not going out today. But you are.'

The next minute this British School of Motoring car showed up. And she said, 'We found a voucher in the paper, so we booked you a lesson. Go!'

What a surprise! I had a great instructor; he was amazing. His name was Bill, and he owned two Morris Minors that he was restoring. He gave me so much extra time and let me play the radio and wear my shades. I passed my test the first time.

After the car accident, I was always drawn to the church, but I didn't know why. I went to the service on Sundays, and I hated it. I just didn't see the point. I was still very young and knew nothing about Spiritualism, so I had no idea this was the reason for my unexplained attraction to the church.

One day, a very well-known medium from Edinburgh came into the café where I worked. Her son had been murdered, and through her ability, she had been able to tell the police who had killed her son, where he was killed and why. She must have recognised something in me because she told me I would be working like her in the future. I thought, *What a load of rubbish*. If only I had listened.

I enjoyed my job, but I still felt I wanted more. Even though I didn't believe in it at that time in my life, the spirit world listened, and I was given guidance.

When I was 19, my late grandfather appeared in front of me, standing at the bottom of my bed. He was wearing his jeans and a white shirt with his red jumper over it and had the biggest smile on his face. He was glowing! He tried to give me advice, and when he said, 'You should be working for the Spirit,' I didn't understand. I thought he meant the alcoholic spirit, and for me, that meant hospitality.

The following night I wasn't sure if I was awake or dreaming, but I saw my Great-Aunt Lizzie, whom I'd never met before. She had tight curls in her hair and her glasses on the end of her nose, and she was a thin, frail lady with defined features, wearing a purple cardigan. She repeated the message my grandfather had given me.

When I told my mother the following day, she said, 'So what, you've seen a ghost; who really cares?' My gran, however, listened but made no comment. I found that a bit strange because my Gran's mother, my Granny Brown, used to read tea leaves, and I thought it was a fun party trick until I realised that this is part of the whole spiritual environment. Maybe my gran was hiding something from me?

Just about that time, Lesley and I parted. It just wasn't going to work out. It was quite sad. She came back into my life very briefly last year when I was doing a show. At first, I didn't recognise her, but by the end of the night, we each realised who the other was. That was funny. And she got a message on the night!

I applied for a job at the Carlton Highland Hotel as a banqueting supervisor, and I was successful. It was a move that would define my working life for the next 20 years.

It was a good job, but I wanted to make more money. I needed to be confident that I would always have enough money for my mortgage because now that I was out, I was never going back home. Not only that, I wanted to have enough left over to enjoy life.

The solution was to sign up with a temp agency. I started working part-time for an agency called Premiere Connections in my downtime from the Carlton. At the time, it was just to make some extra money. Little did I know it would set me on a path that would end with my serving royalty.

In the Carlton Highland, my head got turned by a rather attractive young lady called Sharon, who worked in the pantry. We started seeing each other, and a year later, we got married.

It was quite an occasion. Because I had family connections to Edinburgh through my grandparents, we were allowed to get married in St Giles' Cathedral. We rode through the ancient streets to the cathedral in a horse and carriage. It must have been a real sight!

After the ceremony, we had our reception in the Grosvenor Hotel in Haymarket. It was a great day!

AN EARTHBOUND ANGEL

My friends from work didn't come to the wedding, and I wondered why. I was soon to find out.

We honeymooned in Jamaica and had a fantastic time. When we got back, we left the Carlton together and went to work in the Norton House Hotel outside Edinburgh. I got a better job as head waiter in the restaurant, and Sharon became a receptionist.

Sharon moved into my flat, and even though she wanted her name to be on the deeds, I resisted. Later I would be glad that I did. However, we did buy a car. It was a brand-new Vauxhall Nova Sport.

One night I was on my way home from work when I had a horrible feeling that something was going to happen. As I walked into the flat, I saw that Sharon and some friends were using a Ouija board to try to connect with the afterlife. Suddenly, the room turned stone cold, and one side of our friend's face began to stream with tears. Just the one side. I told them to get the Ouija board out of my house and fast. It went in the bin, but the energy remained in my flat. I didn't know how to get rid of it. It was so cold! Had I known about Spiritualism, I would have known how to change the energy and renew it, but the damage was done.

From that day on, all my old intuition came back, and strange thoughts started coming into my head. This was disturbing, and I began to wonder if I had some sort of ability after all. Sharon had a pack of tarot cards, and one night I thought I would see if I could understand them. I put the cards out, read the meanings, and found I could link them together. But I didn't really believe it. I thought *This is nonsense; this isn't for me.*

If only I had known this was a trigger trying to push me in the right direction.

The next few months passed smoothly enough. I had a wonderful time working at Norton House, and it might have continued if I had not found out that Sharon had been having an affair.

It was less than six months after the wedding. One day at work, one of the chefs came up to me out of the blue and said, 'Can I have a word with you, Graham?'

Of course, I said yes. He continued, 'I can't keep this from you anymore. You're such a nice guy. I have to tell you.'

He had been seeing my wife.

I didn't know what to think. Then I found out she had also been seeing Ali, a friend who worked with us in the restaurant. I confronted him at work, and he knocked me down the stairs.

Now I knew why none of my friends from work had come to my wedding.

Sharon left and took the car with her, but my mother was having none of it. She came to Norton House and got hold of Sharon in the boardroom. She pinned her up against the wall and asked her for the car keys, and told her not to come back. She was getting nothing from me. I was devastated. I thought I had found love, but I had been fooled. And it affected my work. In the end, I had a conversation with the manager, and we agreed it would be traumatic for me to stay there, so I ended up losing my job as well as my wife.

It got worse. Not only did I have no job, but I also found out my now ex-wife had secured tens of thousands of pounds worth of debt on my flat for goods which had all been delivered to her parents. I had no way to pay it all back. The only option I could see was renting my flat out, moving back to my father's house in Port Seton, and looking for work elsewhere. I didn't want this to happen or to be a long-term fix, but I needed a base to store my things.

That was never going to happen. Instead, I decided to make a fresh start and took a live-in job in Aviemore for the winter season.

Before I went to Aviemore, I needed a break and decided to reach out to some people we met in Jamaica. They lived in Canada, so soon, I was off overseas to visit them and escape the realities that lay ahead. We've now been friends for over 30 years and have both been through so much, but I will never lose the love I have for them and Nana. Nana is in her 90s and sharp as a tack. Her husband, Glen, sadly passed a long time ago. I was very fortunate to have been given his cufflinks which I treasure. Glen had such a great sense of humour, even though his life had not been easy. He was a diabetic and had to have his legs amputated and move to live in a care home. When he knew I was coming to visit, he asked if I'd bring him some chocolate, only he ate all six bars in one day and it had a disastrous effect on his bowels. I am still haunted by the image of his mess, which his nurses had to clean up. But this was escapism!

I've been so lucky to have visited Canada over 17 times in my life and to have such loving, supportive friends who stay in touch from afar. When I feel a bit down, I try some meditation and recall the toga parties in Jamaica where we were dancing with snakes on the beach and the beer-drinking contest where I met my friends for the first time. We were outdrunk by Binki, who was in her 70s. She was as dark as the Ace of Spades, while her husband was as pale as milk. She called him her Little Marshmallow, and he called her his beautiful bowl of Brown Sugar. They turned up every day at the pool with a trolley of Red Stripe beers, and Binki would enter drinking competitions, where I came Second, Rob Third, and Binki stole the Crown!

7. BECOMING THE BEST

I spent the winter season in the Coylumbridge Hotel in Aviemore. It was amazing. I went there as the restaurant banquet supervisor. I lived in the management accommodation, and we had no end of parties!

Near the end of the season, the personnel manager called me in, and I thought they were going to let me go, but instead, it was an offer for a job the following season and a request to take her and her husband to Wick so that he could take his exams to become a vet. I was truly honoured and happy to take them as they couldn't drive.

When the winter season finished, I came back home and got a job at the Royal Scot Hotel as a head waiter, and I had a great time. I did very well there. As that season ended and they were letting staff go, the manager of the Coylumbridge wanted me back, so off I went for a second season. It was bittersweet as there had been a huge fire at one of the sister hotels, and my friend had been killed in the fire at Aviemore, which pulled on my heartstrings. I was gutted, and even today, my heart breaks for those poor people who lost their lives on that fateful night.

We had been out in the village having a few beers before going back to our cottages for Hogmanay in December 1994. We said our 'Goodnights', and the group broke up, and I was heading back to our accommodation because I was on the breakfast shift for the morning of New Year's Day. I knew something didn't feel right, but I put it down to the drink and the feeling I got from changes at work with people coming and going. I woke during the night as if I was choking, but after a coughing fit, I went back to sleep. As I woke the following day, I heard a commotion, with people saying that The Four Seasons was on fire in Aviemore Centre. My heart sank, and I knew I'd never see my good friend again. He died of smoke inhalation. All my intuition came flooding back. I knew this time when I went home I wasn't coming back to Aviemore.

Instead, I came back to the Royal Scot for the summer season – déjà vu! But when that season ended, there was a big financial scandal. Some senior managers kept ex-members of staff on the payroll and took the money for themselves. I was one of those listed. I had queried my payslip because I hadn't been taken off the payroll. Unbeknown to me, this was already being investigated.

My boss called me up for a chat, and I was worried about what that meant. He asked me to speak to Mr B, and I thought this was another ending. But he was about to take a manager's job in Carlisle and wanted me to go with him because of my ability to finesse and complete things. Of course, I agreed and soon left to live in Carlisle, leaving my flat, apart from coming home on my days off.

I worked briefly in Carlisle, but I missed home. Some of my friends worked in the Hunting Tower in Perth, and it sounded all right, so I got a job there. I became an assistant manager, but that just meant I did everything. I did the restaurant, I did the bar, I did the reception. After two years of this, my boss gave me housekeeping to manage too, and I thought, *He hates me, he wants rid of me.*

I was wrong. He had understood that with a strong figurehead, you can achieve anything, and he had recognised that in me.

The hotel had been struggling and losing tens of thousands of pounds yearly, but I was on fire. In their first year, I helped them turn that deficit around into tens of thousands of pounds *of profit*. I did that while travelling from Edinburgh every single day.

After three very happy years, I realised there was no progression route for me there. I was ambitious, so it was time to move on. After a few brief weeks in a hotel on Wester Ross, which wasn't for me, I got a job as the deputy manager of the Invercauld Arms in Braemar.

I got there the week before the Braemar Highland Games when the hotel was at its busiest. I didn't have a clue what was going on. The night porter was leaving, the restaurant manager was leaving… It was horrendous. The day I arrived, the general manager Hans handed me the keys and said, 'I'm going off sick. I've had a nervous breakdown. By the way, we've got a new junior assistant coming on board. Her name is Caroline.'

Caroline duly arrived. She seemed nice, and luckily we got along because we were basically the management. This meant we worked closely together, and our work relationship naturally developed into something more personal. In Hospitality, it was the norm that management and staff didn't mix because of the mere structure of giving orders. Being in a relationship with a colleague was frowned upon, regardless of the position or department. If you were found out, you would be paid off and let go without further explanation.

Eventually, the work situation at the Invercauld Arms became too much. I knew I wasn't ready to be a General Manager, but I saw myself as a good deputy. The Invercauld had just been sold to another group, and it might be months before a new General Manager came to post. I knew I couldn't continue there, and I started looking for something else. I applied for the deputy manager's position at the Cartland Bridge Hotel in Lanark, and I got it.

It was a live-in position. I expected it would be hard to tell Caroline I was leaving because we had grown so close. I hoped we would keep in touch. But when I eventually told her, she surprised me. She said, 'Could I come with you?'

Without really thinking, I replied, 'Well, I'm going to live in Lanark, so you can stay in my flat, and I'll travel back on my days off.'

And that was what we did. It was nice to have someone to come home to and to be part of a relationship again. I thought it must be love. During this time, there had been the most awful storm, and the roof of my hotel had been damaged, along with a loss of power. There was no way I was getting home to Edinburgh. So I called my mother and discovered that they were all ill, along with my stepfather. Caroline duly went and looked after them until they were strong enough to look after themselves while I attended to the hotel in Lanark.

I lasted a year and a half in Lanark before I decided to go back to Perth. I never really liked living away from home. I always liked coming back to my own place and could travel to Perth from home.

Then came a big opportunity.

There was to be a new hotel near the Palace of Holyroodhouse. It would be one of the most prestigious five-star hotels to open in Edinburgh, and I was offered the role of deputy manager. I jumped at the chance.

It was 1999 when we started interviewing for staff for the Holyrood Hotel. The management team were put in place first so we could organise the marketing and agree on the design of the building and how things would be set out.

Caroline, meanwhile, was ready to move our relationship to the next level. She said, 'If this relationship is going to work, we're going to have to buy somewhere else. Somewhere that is ours.'

I wasn't sure at first. I loved my flat, and I wasn't quite ready to part with it. Eventually, we agreed that we would buy somewhere else, and I would rent out my flat.

A new housing estate was being built not far from the flat, so I went to see if there were any houses available. I was lucky. A sale had fallen through on a two-bedroom house, and I could have it right away.

I gave the house to Caroline on Valentine's Day. I took her out in the car without telling her where we were going. I drove the short distance to the new house and stopped outside it. I shone the light through the window and said, 'That's your new house!'

She loved it from the start. We moved there in March 2000. We took that house to bits and worked on it together until we got it the way we wanted it. It was stunning.

Meanwhile, the plans for the opening of Holyrood were well underway. We opened there in August 2000. We did this whole marketing thing about 'Hollywood comes to Holyrood', which was partly my idea. That got us on the six o'clock news, and publicity kept the hotel busy.

Despite the success of the hotel, all was not going well for me. My boss kept trying to get rid of me, and although it took me a while, I finally worked out he was jealous of me. He sent me to another hotel in the chain, but they didn't have the budget for me, so he had no choice but to take me back. It made for a difficult working environment.

Luckily it was all about to change. My old boss at Hunting Tower phoned to tell me they had just bought a hotel in Edinburgh, and would I be interested in going back to work for him?

I jumped at it. I met him at the Balmoral for coffee to sort out the details, and then I went back to Holyrood and handed in my notice.

The new hotel was called Simpson's. It was on the site of the very first maternity hospital in Edinburgh, which was opened during the war. It was named after James Young Simpson, who was the pioneer of chloroform.

In fact, they used to have chloroform parties in the basement, my new reception. All my fears came flooding back because it was so creepy walking the floors of this hotel and seeing faces or shadows as I looked back, and I didn't know who or what they were. It was intriguing but frightening.

This got worse when I was on jury service and had to pop back into work afterwards. I kept getting visions of a ferry and a bag dropping overboard. I had no idea why. When I went back to the hotel after jury service, this guest asked if I could get a weekend break for him and his partner, and it turned out he worked for Seacat, a ferry company, and he was in Edinburgh to give evidence at the Limbs in the Loch case, where the body parts were washed up on Barassie Beach. This was the case I'd been on as jury spokesperson. I couldn't tell my guest this, and he never was called to give evidence, but all the witnesses from the Seacat company ended up staying at the hotel after the case closed. Then I was able to reveal that I'd been on the jury and helped sort out the gentlemen's weekend trip, and in return, he arranged a crossing for myself and my then-wife to visit Ireland.

It was great at the hotel, but it was a very old building and, besides, it had been a hospital. People had died there. Back came all the spiritual stuff. I felt people around me all the time. I felt them following me, but no one was there when I turned. It got so bad I didn't want to be left alone.

Despite that, I turned it into a four-star hotel within six months. It was my first general management position, and I was determined to make it work. It had 56 bedrooms, including suites, plus a restaurant and bar. A lot of attention to detail was needed, but that's what I was renowned for – my finishes and my attention to detail. I put in the standards that needed to be in place and met all my targets. I was even recognised in the Edinburgh Evening News for my efforts.

8. TOASTMASTER TO THE QUEEN

Even though I was working in full-time roles and senior positions, I still took on temporary work for Premiere Connections and other agencies whenever possible.

There were five of us working for them in Edinburgh who became very, very good at what we did. We became known unofficially as the A-Team, and together we could do the work of ten. Whenever the five of us were posted together, the organisers knew we would carry the room. Clients would even ask if the A-Team was available when they were booking their events.

Being one of the best, I was trusted to attend events that important people and even celebrities attended. I was often posted to Murrayfield Stadium, which is the home of Scottish Rugby, and eventually, it became a regular event for me. If Murrayfield had a function on and I was able to do it, I would be there.

At that time, Lord Younger was the chairman of The Royal Bank of Scotland, which sponsored Scottish Rugby, and Princess Anne was the patron, so whenever they were present at a match, I would get the job of looking after the table. Lord Younger and his wife were always very kind to me.

I used to bank in St Andrews Square, where Lord Younger had his office. Once in a while, if Lord Younger saw me there, he would take the time to chat with me and perhaps even offer me a quick coffee. It wasn't a regular thing, but it was really nice. It was very touching.

In 1995, I was posted to Holyrood Palace to cover a big dinner dance that was being held there in aid of a charity. It was exciting because members of the Royal Family would be attending. As staff, we were not supposed to use the main door. We had to go in through the windows of the ballroom. Everything we needed had to come in that way, too, because it was a working palace, and we were on the clock as it was about to close to the public.

Of course, all of the staff had to be vetted beforehand to make sure we didn't pose a threat to the royal family. Despite this, the person who was supposed to run the function was turned back at the gate and refused entry. This was because, during his national service in France 35 years before, he and his friend had got drunk and driven a tank around the army barracks. That meant he was perceived to be a threat to the Queen. At the time, we all thought it was funny, but it just goes to show how seriously they took it.

I was given the job of running the function, and we began the setup. That was the important part. Soon the tables were laid, and there were only some menial things left to do before the pre-event briefing, like setting up the drinks reception.

I had the job of setting up the drinks reception in the throne room, which was where the guests would arrive. Now, when a member of the royal family comes downstairs into the throne room, all the doors close at once for security reasons. A High Constable with a baton and top hat is stationed inside the door, but an armed officer from the Queen's Own Regiment is on the other side.

I was busy setting up the reception when suddenly – *slam* – went the doors. At once, I stopped what I was doing and turned around. It was the Queen Mother!

She walked towards me, and I did the courteous thing and bowed. She stopped in front of me and asked, 'What is this evening's event?'

I replied, 'It's a dinner dance, Your Majesty.'

She said to me, 'A dinner dance?'

'Yes, Ma'am.'

She then said, 'Do you know how to dance in a style that I would be accustomed to?'

She meant ballroom dancing. Surreal as it was, she got me in frame, and she and I took three steps together in the throne room. Then she did whatever it was she had originally come to do and left, and I had literally six minutes to get from the throne room to the main ballroom ready for our briefing.

After the drinks reception, dinner was served. I was the lead in that room, and every member of staff was watching me. The signal was given to begin service.

The starters were done and cleared with no problems. It was time for the main course.

AN EARTHBOUND ANGEL

I'm left-handed, which can make silver service a bit awkward, and I was holding this massive ceramic chafing dish filled with sirloin steaks on my arm. There were 12 people on that top table, which was quite a lot for one person to do. I, however, was an expert.

First, I served the Queen and Prince Philip, then I worked my way down the table until I got to Princess Anne. She had decided to chat to someone next to her, so she had her body turned away. As I went in to serve, I said, 'Good evening, Your Royal Highness.'

I got no response. I then said, 'Good evening, Ma'am.'

Still no response. The whole room was waiting for me to finish. I thought *I'll just go for it.*

As I did, she suddenly turned and nudged the dish on my arm. The gravy slopped over the side onto my white gloves. Quickly I tried to juggle the dish so that the remaining sirloins didn't go all over Princess Anne. Oh, that would have been a story for the press if it had happened! Luckily, I held on, and my reputation was saved!

As part of my regular job, I worked at a lot of weddings – sometimes almost 200 a year – and part of the job was to be the toastmaster, the person responsible for proposing toasts, introducing speakers, and making other formal announcements.

As I gained more experience, I did weddings for celebrities and other public figures. Donald Dewar was the inaugural First Minister of Scotland, and it was after I did his daughter's wedding that I received a call from an agent on behalf of St. James's Palace. I could hardly believe it. They asked me if I would consider joining the team and becoming a Toastmaster to the Queen.

That job is done by a small, select group of people, and they cover different regions of the country. If the family were in the Central Belt of Scotland, I'd be asked to look after them.

The rules were very simple. You would turn up, you would go in, you would do the job, and you would leave.

Of course, I had to sign the Official Secrets Act at the time, so I couldn't officially disclose what I was doing to anyone.

In 1999, the Roxburgh Hotel had just re-launched, and the owner wanted to put on a big event. Princess Anne was going to be in Scotland, and he thought he could invite her to open it. Word came back that she would do it on behalf of the Princess Royal Trust for Carers.

I was asked if I could do the event for him. I had to say no as a third party on behalf of St James had already booked me for it, which I couldn't disclose to him because I would have broken the Official Secrets Act. That would have been treason. He threatened to sack me if I didn't do the event, but what could I do?

On the night, of course, I turned up and looked after the table. That caused a bit of friction, but really, I had no choice. After dinner, Princess Anne was ready to leave. I moved her chair back for her. She stood, turned to me, and said, 'Thank you,' as she always did.

I said, 'Good evening, Ma'am,' and she left.

By the time she was saying her goodbyes at the front door, I was already back in the car and on my way home. That's how it worked.

I did hundreds of events for the Royal Family over the 16 years I served them. It's not something I've talked much about. In my time, I've met most of the senior royals. I've met Diana, Charles, Andrew, the Queen and Philip, of course, and Edward and Sophie.

William and Harry were only kids at the time, so I didn't really have anything to do with them, but Diana would regularly come down to the staff chambers at the palace, and there were several conversations I was party to when she was there. I thought she was lovely. Certainly, when she came down into the staff quarters, you could tell she was a lady who was very unhappy.

I was so stunned when the news broke of her death. I was leaving the house to drive to Perth, and the tears just started to flow, and shivers ran through my body.

It really did touch a nerve. Having met her and knowing that she was lovely, it was phenomenal when it later turned out to be her who first connected me to the spirit world proper. I often think about that.

But the royal family are not strangers to the spiritual movement. The Queen Mother was known to turn to mediums after the death of her husband. She became friends with a medium called Lilian Bailey, and they struck up a fabulous friendship.

One very famous time, Lilian was asked to do a group sitting, which she never wanted to do. Eventually, she said yes. She was blindfolded and taken to a secret location, which turned out to be, I believe, Kensington or Buckingham Palace. She could hear the rustles of the clothes of the sitters coming in. And when she removed her blindfold, there was the Queen Mother, the Queen, Princess Margaret and the Duke and Duchess of Kent.

Later, the Queen Mother wanted to give Lilian something to say thank you for being there for her when she was grieving. Most of the jewels she had belonged to the Crown, but she found a beautiful brooch that her late husband had given her, and the next time she met Lilian, she pinned it on Lilian's left lapel. That was the last time they met in this world because they both passed away shortly after. I'm sure they would have been reunited in the spirit world.

When I met the Queen Mother, she was still grieving the death of her husband, even though he had passed almost half a century ago. I think that's why there was a pull between us, and we ended up having a conversation. It was very touching. Grieving was difficult for her because she was in the public eye. It's a very difficult role, and I don't know if I could have coped with that amount of intrusion.

It was the same for Prince William when he was at university in St Andrews. I spent some time working at the nearby Bar, part of the Festival Portfolio, so I was there when William and Catherine Middleton (now the Princess of Wales) were socialising together. Any bar that William wanted to drink in had to be approved in advance, and he was always accompanied by his security detail. He would be sitting at one table, and his security team would be nearby, ready to act.

I am discreet about my connection with the Royal Family, but I have a reminder in my home: a gift from the royal family for my service. It is an ornament shaped like a double inverted geometric quartz triangle with a blue onyx world globe on which the continents are depicted in gold leaf. I was given that for my service and will always treasure it.

Working in hospitality was a wonderful life, and I was good at what I did. It was one of the most humbling professions I could ever have chosen, and I always gave it my best. To do it, I had to be on top of my game, and that was recognised. I was awarded 'Employee of the Year' many times, and I was promoted right to the top.

9. TRAGEDY STRIKES

As I have gone through my life, I have always craved the affection that was lacking when I was young. Because of that, I have accepted love (or what I thought was love) wherever it could be found.

I believe that is why I jumped into marriage with Sharon. I thought it was love, but I was wrong. After our divorce, I said I would never get married again. Never. But that vow was made to be broken.

Caroline was much younger than me, and my friends didn't like her. Neither did the neighbours, though I got on with them very well. Perhaps I should have paid heed.

One day, in February 2002, I came home from work as usual, and as I was heading upstairs, Caroline shouted a question to me. I didn't hear what she said, and I replied, 'Yes.'

Then I realised what she had said. It was, 'Will you marry me?'

My heart sank, but I couldn't understand why. I thought I really loved her and, if that was true, I would want to get married. Wouldn't I?

She was already on the phone with her mother, telling her the news, and I could hear the excitement in her voice. The rollercoaster was starting up again, and I didn't know how to get off. I knew in my heart that getting married was wrong for both of us, but there had been so much turmoil in my life already that I didn't want to cause any more.

All the old fears came rushing back. If I went to her and said, 'No,' would I lose the love I thought I had found? Would I be alone again? If that happened, I would surely return to that dark place where I only wanted to escape this life. And I didn't want to be there, either.

As we got closer and closer to the day, the feeling of dread grew stronger. I knew I should do something, but I couldn't find the will to stop it. I did try. Shortly before the wedding, I said to my best man, 'I don't want to do this.'

He thought it was just nerves. Besides, we were too far down the line by then. There was too much invested in it. Perhaps I just wasn't mature enough to say, 'I'm really sorry, I don't want to do this. Can we just stop?'

Even if I had, would anyone have listened?

We got married in Autumn 2002. It was a massive wedding. We were married in St Giles' Cathedral, the same venue as my first wedding, and there were four limos lined up outside for the wedding party. Japanese tourists were taking pictures!

The reception was held in the Royal Terrace Hotel, and that was fabulous. Then we went to Thailand for our honeymoon.

Despite my misgivings, I found I was quite settled in my life at this point. We wanted a family. We were sure Caroline had fallen pregnant in December, only three months after we married. I began to think that maybe I could be happy after all.

Fate, of course, had other ideas. Caroline miscarried just before Christmas. It felt like the end of the world, but worse was to come. Something that would change my life forever.

January 5, 2003, had been a strange day. I had known something wasn't right all day, but I just couldn't put my finger on what it could be. I thought it might be work, but I was wrong.

At nine o'clock at night, I was in the shower when the phone rang downstairs. As soon as I heard it ring, the feeling intensified inside me. This was it, and it would be bad.

Caroline brought the phone up to me. It was my stepmother. Caroline held the phone up, and I could hear my stepmother, but I could barely make out what she was saying. I thought she had been drinking. I told Caroline, 'Tell her I'll call her back.'

Caroline shook her head. 'She wants to speak to you right now.'

I had no idea what could be so urgent that it couldn't wait a few minutes. However, I stepped out of the shower and took the phone. Without any warning, my stepmother said, 'Garry is dead. You'd better come home.'

I dropped the phone, and it clattered on the bathroom floor. I could barely comprehend what I had been told. It was surreal. Somehow, I dressed and headed to my father's house. There we were told my brother had been found hanging in his office.

At the time, I didn't quite understand the extent of what had gone on, but in the years that followed, I learned that my brother had been involved in dealing drugs, and the bank was about to close on him for fraud. He couldn't cope. Worse, it turned out that the drug dealers were people I knew.

I was so lost. My brother was gone.

That was also the start of the long road to disaster for our marriage.

We were typical brothers, Garry and me. We didn't see a lot of each other, and we weren't friends. In fact, he hated me with a passion. I'd never understood why, but after his death, his partner told me he was jealous of the relationship I had with my mother and my professional achievements.

I found that hard to understand because, in my mind, he had achieved so much himself. He had children, which I didn't get to have, and I was envious of that, but to him, I had the relationships he wanted and couldn't have. I had so much regret for what might have been.

He had tried to take his own life before, but he had been stopped. I found out he had tried to get help: he had gone to his doctor three times, but they had turned him away. They told him to come back after Christmas. He had told them he was going to kill himself, and they turned him away.

I had to arrange the funeral with my grieving father by my side because my mother and father were overwhelmed with grief. He lay at the undertaker's for three weeks after his death, and many people came to view him. I had to eventually ask for the lid to be put on the coffin.

The funeral was huge. I nearly fell into the grave. I've never been so lost and distressed in all my life. The realisation that my younger brother had died was too huge to deal with.

It was very emotional. My parents were distraught. Those memories don't go away, and even now, I get emotional even thinking about it. I had a friend through work who had florists, and I had her arrange the flowers for my brother's funeral, and they said I could come in if I wanted, so for a few days, I prepared the flowers for my brother's farewell. I helped create a mass of white flowers like a carpet arrangement, and the florist did the small focal points on each arrangement. But they encouraged me to feel free to help out in the future.

We went through a whole six months of grieving. It was one of the worse periods of my life. In those six months, a close relative of Caroline's also died, and my gran's health deteriorated. I was at the Royal Infirmary with her when they told her she had cancer in her kidneys and that she needed surgery. My grandmother was my life. I could not contemplate going on without her. The one spark of light in all this was that she survived the cancer.

We went through a whole six months of that. One trauma after another. Every day I woke up and thought, *What next?*

One day, I offered to take a spin dryer to the recycling centre for the neighbours. Carelessly I slipped on the path, and the spin dryer landed on top of me. Pain shot through my back. When I finally got to my feet, I could hardly walk. The

GP told me I had pulled a muscle, but I knew he was wrong. I had no idea how bad it was going to get.

It was all too much. I had to give up work. I couldn't cope. The trauma of loss was horrendous. It was horrific.

I became very depressed. I took to sitting at my brother's grave, and it would just break my heart. Then I would make excuses for where I had been. I didn't know what was going on, so how could I explain it to anybody else? I didn't tell Caroline that I was sitting at my brother's grave. I would probably have been sectioned. My mother-in-law came to visit and handed me a book from the church about Grief. This was the last thing I needed, and I couldn't understand what was going on. I wanted out, but my brother had left instead, leaving me behind. Why didn't he just talk to me? All of these things had been going around in my head, and I just wanted to be left in my own bubble.

Other things started to happen. Men kept approaching me in the street, trying to pick me up, and I couldn't understand why. I had never been attracted to men. It became a real problem, and I started to question myself.

I started to see people who weren't there. I found myself talking to people who didn't exist but who were real to me. I wanted my life to end. I had no idea how to cope with what my life was becoming. Neither did Caroline, and that worried her.

My mental health was in a terrible state. Every day I struggled to function, trying to put a face on for the world. When I went to discuss it with my GP, I wasn't very honest with him because I knew what he would do. I knew I would have been referred to the Royal Edinburgh Infirmary because he had already told me that's what he would do if I developed psychosis. And what other name would they give it? I was talking to thin air.

I was diagnosed with clinical depression.

I think that was partly why our marriage ended up falling apart. I couldn't discuss any of this with Caroline because I didn't know what was going on, and it must have been difficult for her not to know what was happening. I began to withdraw from her because I really started to think *I can't continue to be close to her. Because I'm not staying in this world.*
I'm ready to leave it.

10. MY INTUITION RETURNS

In May 2003, I decided that no matter what was happening in my head, I needed to return to work. I needed to get back to something I could control. Besides, there was a mortgage to be paid, and I couldn't lose the house.

As I was looking for work, I took up my friend's offer to help at their florist, either delivering or helping with arrangements or even just chatting for however long I wanted. Soon I was asked to help them close a shop in Livingston and transfer the business to Edinburgh. The partner was considering opening a bigger shop which I advised against, although I wasn't sure why. I even invested in it while I was looking for another job. Things seemed okay, but I had a bad feeling about it, and I was right. The partner had no control over her spending, and the business went under.

I had replied to an advertisement for London and Edinburgh Inns, which was to become Swallow Hotels. There was nothing in Scotland at the time, but later they called and asked if I would be interested in going to a hotel in Kent. I agreed to go and troubleshoot as the general manager.

I flew home every second week, or Caroline sometimes came down to see me in Kent instead.

Strange things happened in that hotel. It was rumoured that it was haunted by a chambermaid who had died there, and I'm sure I saw her on more than one occasion. I often heard her walking in the corridors, but when I looked, there was nobody there.

Part of the hotel was used for polling on election days. One time, everything had been set up the night before but when we turned up the following morning, everything was scattered all over the floor, as if a child had been in and thrown it all about.

I worked there for the rest of 2003 and returned home at Christmas. After that, I was offered the general manager's role in a four-star hotel in Symington, Lanarkshire, that was being added to the Swallow portfolio. Could I take it on and make it work? Of course, I could.

My intuition was beginning to kick in again. In May 2005, a woman called Emma Caldwell from Glasgow was murdered. The police search had moved to Lanarkshire, and the investigation team stayed at my hotel.

Somehow, I knew she was in the woods in Lanarkshire. I didn't know why. I didn't even know her name at that point; I was just sensing something. I had no idea where the feeling came from. Had I heard someone say Emma or not?

I knew what I was getting was the truth. But how could I tell that to somebody? I had no evidence. I just knew. It was as if she was talking to me and telling me where she was. I forced myself to tell the police, but the woodland was so vast I mistook the area, and nothing came of it.

It went to the back of my mind until I saw on the news that she had been found in those woods, not far from where I had sensed her.

Around the same time, I had a feeling that a company I had shares in was about to go under. I sensed that something would happen, and everything would be gone. Sure enough, shortly after that, the owner's son's business was destroyed in a fire. Everything was gone, just as I had foreseen.

It had been a sketchy feeling, not a defined thought at all, but I knew I was becoming better at tuning into it. I just didn't know why. I couldn't process what was happening. I was still seeing people and hearing voices. In fact, they were becoming clearer. I began to wonder if I was schizophrenic.

I did a good job in Symington, and I moved to the Ramada Hotel in Edinburgh with a view to staying there as general manager. I had become a trouble-shooter for the company, turning underperforming hotels into money-makers again. In fact, it was noted that I was the *only* manager at that time to be making any money.

Work was my life, and I knew I was good at my job, but throughout my career, I had to cope with the jealousy of other people. Because of that I was continually moved on or let go. I couldn't understand why because I did nothing wrong. All I did was work my socks off for the company. Then they would say, 'Sorry, we're going to have to let you go.'

It didn't make sense. It knocked my confidence every time, but it was the only industry I knew, and I just had to pick myself up and start again every time.

Now, later in life, I believe that all the signs were there. No matter how good I was at my job, it was not where I was meant to be, and there was a reason I was constantly being moved on. I should have been working for Spirit because I always knew it was coming. I just refused to acknowledge it.

11. THE END OF THE BEGINNING

Life became very hard. Being approached and harassed by other men was getting worse and worse. I became very distressed, and I was starting to get into fights. I was looking for ways and means of trying to let everything out without knowing why or what was changing. Perhaps I put myself in slightly dangerous situations because I wanted out of this life and all the problems I had. But how could I tell that to anybody? I just couldn't.

Something was changing. Not physically, but mentally or emotionally. Something was going on. I was becoming much more sensitive than I had ever been, and I didn't know why. My dreams became quite distressing.

Now, much later in my life, I know that the masculine and feminine energy was starting to bring balance to my mind to prepare me for the work I was to do. If only I had understood, but there was no one I could discuss it with.

Caroline's response to all of this was that we should move house and that I was the problem.

There was a house on Glasgow Road that we used to pass every time we went to visit my mother. It had been up for sale for a while, and every time we passed it, I had the sense that this was the house we would be living in. The only thing was, it was too expensive, so we looked elsewhere.

In 2004, we bought a house near Dalmahoy. I sensed that we wouldn't be moving into it, but I couldn't understand why. I found out on Christmas Eve on our way to visit my mother. Our solicitor called to tell us the sale had fallen through. By this point, our old house had been sold, and we were left with nowhere to go.

As we drove along Glasgow Road, we passed that house again. After discussing things with my mother, she decided to phone the number on the schedule, and we arranged to see it on the way home. What did we have to lose?

As soon as I stepped inside, I knew this was the house for me. We had a look around, saw what we could do with it, and talked the owner down to a price we could afford. He must have liked us because, as we were talking, I noticed a beautiful slate Mantel Clock on the ledge upstairs, and before I knew it this elderly lady had carried it downstairs and given it to me as a gift! I thought she was going to fall or hurt herself as she carried this heavy clock into the room. I was very touched and honoured that they gave this to me. We used to joke that it was a bribe, but it certainly wasn't. After all, I negotiated a huge discount on the house after we had it surveyed, and we offered what we'd agreed for the house.

The house was surveyed on December 27, and we finally got an entry date of March 3, 2005. I felt like I was coming home.

That was something positive in a very bleak time. However, my health was suffering. The injury to my back was getting worse, but it wasn't a constant pain. Some days I was doubled over in agony, but other days I was fine. Some days I could hardly walk. Caroline didn't understand how I could be fine one day and not the next. She was getting more and more fed up. and there was nothing I could do about it.

Around September, I went to a weight-loss clinic with a view to seeing if it managed my pain, and when I was there, I realised I could do everything they did myself. As I left, I knew I was about to open a business.

In late 2005, I opened what became known as The Body Toning Clinic. Caroline chose the name. It was an alternative health and beauty clinic. Her father made a wee sign for the gatepost, and we started working from the two upstairs bedrooms of our house. We also had a bit of space in the attic that I used as a wee office. It didn't take off initially; it was very slow to get going.

It was becoming more and more difficult to disguise the pain in my back. At a wedding previously, a guest had noticed I was suffering, and she asked, 'Have you got problems with your back?'

I had to admit I did. She had a friend who worked at Edinburgh Royal Infirmary, and she got me an appointment. The friend took one look at me and said, 'Just stay where you are. I need a surgeon to see you.' It turned out that when I had fallen, I had taken a chip out of my spine and damaged two nerves. I would need surgery for a fusion and disc compression.

It was planned for October 2005, but that clashed with our planned holiday, so I had to reschedule. When we came back from that holiday, Caroline announced she was leaving me.

She said she was going to stay with a friend from work, so she would take a few things and go.

After all that had happened, it didn't really surprise me.

I finally went for surgery in 2006. What should have been a simple operation turned out to be a nightmare.

I went in for the spinal fusion and disk compression, but, after surgery, when they tried to get me up out of bed, I couldn't walk. I had no feeling in my right foot or ankle, and I had something they described as 'drop foot'. They put me in a chair, which I later found out was a mistake.

It got worse. I didn't have any feeling in my toes either. The following day, I was taken back to the theatre, but it was too late. I should have been taken back the same day. That was followed by a third operation in quick succession.

These operations were to find out why I wasn't recovering. I don't really remember much about it all because I was on drugs to manage my pain.

I found out much later what had happened. During the first operation, instrumentation had been put down on my nerve for about two minutes and thirty seconds. That was enough to damage the nerve forever. I also found out it wasn't the surgeon who did the whole operation. His chief registrar did half of it.

There was a fourth operation. Then the surgeon went on compassionate leave, and my mother went ballistic at his locum. She told him she was going to the press because they had got it so wrong.

I was in the Royal Infirmary for four months. Shortly after I got home, I fell, and I was taken back to the hospital, this time to St. John's in Livingstone.

While I was in the hospital, my estranged wife offered to come back and help look after me. I needed constant care, so the agreement was that my mum would look after me during the day, and my estranged wife would take over at night. When she came back, she moved into what had been our dining room.

Right from the start, she treated me like dirt. Then someone who I thought was my friend came to see me. He invited us over to his house, and when we were there, I realised he and Caroline were together. That made me wonder why she had come back at all. I would soon find out.

Things between us became extremely fraught. Then my in-laws turned up at the house with my wife's new boyfriend. I knew something was wrong and with no one else to turn to, I called my mother. I was right. They had come to empty the house. They knew I could do nothing to stop them. In all the confusion, I had a fall, and they refused to let me call an ambulance. All I could do was lie there and pray someone would turn up to help.

Help came in the shape of my mother and the police, whom she had called on the way. My mother hauled my wife out of the house, and the police told her to go.

An ambulance was called, and I was rushed back to the hospital under police escort in case the metal in my back had moved. If it had, I would have been paralysed for life.

I was then transferred to the spinal rehabilitation unit at Astley Ainslie Hospital in Edinburgh, where I spent two or three months in recovery. I wasn't well enough to work, and I had to resign my post.

That hurt. I was known for my brand, and, as a manager, I made money. That was the one thing I never failed at. I always met my targets. I never overspent when I didn't have to, and I knew the business inside out. It was what I had done all my life, and now it looked as if it was over.

Patients in recovery were allowed home visits, but every time I asked if I could come home, my family and friends changed the subject, and no one ever visited for very long. I started to wonder what they were keeping from me.

Finally, my mother agreed to bring me home for the day, but there was something she had to tell me first. While I was in the hospital, my estranged wife and her boyfriend turned up at the house at five o'clock in the morning and picked the locks on the front door. They had come to clear out the house again, and this time they had succeeded. The neighbour saw them leaving at about six thirty and tried to call my mother, but it was too late.

When we arrived at the house, I was both excited and upset. My mother and I discussed why this had been kept from me, and she said it was because the best place for me had been the hospital and if I'd thought the house would get emptied, I would have discharged myself. This thought had crossed my mind several times whilst in Astley Ainslie. Once we got out of the car and headed up the path, my mother opened the door, and I heard the words 'Welcome home, Graham.' I looked at my mother and said, 'Who's here?' She replied, confused, 'No one?' I heard something again, but she didn't seem to hear it. Then I sent her out of the house and went to the back door to see if this was a prank. But the voice spoke again, saying, 'I said, Welcome home Graham.' Was this finally the spirit looking after me? I still didn't know, and I think my mother thought I was crazy, as she didn't hear a thing.

Although I knew the house had been emptied, nothing could have prepared me for the devastation I felt when I saw it. The house was literally empty. There was nothing left but a broken bed. My antique clocks, my TV, all the special mementoes from my career – all gone. She had left me one fork, one knife, one spoon, one cup and one plate. She had taken everything else.

My now estranged wife came to me with nothing, but when she left, she wanted everything. While in the hospital, I learned she had all my antiques and even my sports car valued. Now I knew why she had come back to me at all.

During this time, the business was just getting going, and Caroline seemed to think I was making a lot of money from it. My mother became involved in the business, and in 2007, we moved it out of the house and into a shop across the road. All the leases and everything were put in my mother's name. and it began to do very well.

I bought a Porsche. It was an older model, and I put the private plate on it that I'd got for my birthday. I was lucky enough to get it very cheaply from someone who was getting divorced and didn't want his wife to get the car. I could sympathise!

Caroline saw all of this, and she wanted part of it. Then the court battle started.

I was very ill, but I wasn't going to give up. She had not contributed a penny to the house all the time she had lived there. I was determined to protect my assets, but the law was on her side. The court awarded her half of absolutely everything. It amounted to tens of thousands of pounds.

I had no idea how to raise the money to pay her. At one point, I thought I would have to sell the house, but luckily, I managed to keep it, with a lot of financial help and support from my mother, who loaned me part of the monies to be paid.

By 2008, my mother was running the business. It was just the two of us by then, and it was so nice. Despite the occasional falling out, we had become very close. That was all about to change once more.

My mother was on holiday in Spain, and I was minding the shop. The phone rang, and I answered it, thinking it was a client. It was the police. They wanted to speak to me about a historic matter. Could we arrange an interview?

I had no idea what it was about. How could I? If I had suspected the truth, I would have been horrified.

They took me to a police station and interviewed me under caution. At that interview, they alleged that I had abused my stepbrother when I lived with my mother and stepfather (when I was only 13 or 14). I was numb with shock. How could I be accused of such a thing? Suddenly, all the memories of the abuse that *I* had suffered came rushing back.

My stepfather had given the police a statement. In it, he said that my mother wished I had never been born. That she had never loved me or wanted me and that she couldn't wait to get rid of me – I was like a noose around her neck, he claimed. He went on to say that he had never wanted me either, and if he could have, he would have ditched me so that my mother could just be with him. He never loved me, and I caused only problem after problem for him.

I couldn't hold back the tears. It all came tumbling out of me. Everything I had suffered, everything that had happened to me when I was a child and since.

The police realised what was going on. They realised I wasn't the problem. They started asking for details of my historic abuse, but by then, I had had enough. I couldn't cope. I was so distressed that they stopped the interview and took me home.

The first thing I did when I got home was to call my mother in Spain. I told her about the statement and asked her what was going on.

She claimed she didn't know, but I think she was lying. Then she told me, 'You can't come to our house anymore. Because you will kill him.'

And I would have. I would have.

This was a man I had learned to tolerate. One night in particular that I remember, he told me that his relationship with my mother was one of convenience, not of love. He said she bought my love. I was so angry, and I tried to tell my mother, but she said she wouldn't leave him and end up with nothing again. It was clear from then on that money was her driver, and she did buy love, but not from her children, just from anywhere outside her family. As much as it pained me, this man was being truthful about my mother. But I can't excuse his behaviour or the part he played in the lies that ensued and the statement he gave. Karma will catch up with him; it will bite him and bite hard.

My mother said she would deal with it when she came back. When I hung up, she was all I could think about. I turned our relationship over and over in my head. She had abandoned me when I was 14, even though she knew what my father was like. She didn't turn up when they thought I was dying after my car accident, and then she thought she could step back into my life in my twenties. I thought she probably knew all about this mess with my stepfather. But why did she behave this way? All I had ever done was to be good to her.

Our relationship changed forever that day.

All those negative feelings that I hoped had gone away had come back with a vengeance. I didn't want to be here in this life. Again, I felt there was someone following me. And I thought, *Who's following me now?*

I think it must have been some sort of protection. Someone watching over me through all the bad times, but I didn't know it then. It just made me afraid.

I felt so lonely. I felt that I just wasn't wanted. It was so bad.

Despite all the upset, my mother and I were still in business together. I had to work with her daily with all these negative feelings inside me. By this time, we had expanded to six clinics, and we had 17 staff working for us.

In January 2009, we had a major flood in the shops in Hamilton and Edinburgh. I knew the business might struggle, so I paid for everything and put the cost on my credit card while we waited for the insurance money. But it never came.

In the summer of 2009, my mother was taking me shopping, and we got into a fight. It was the last straw. I had tried to cling to the remains of what we had, but I could take no more. When she stopped at the traffic lights, I undid the seatbelt and got out of the car. I could barely walk, but there was no way I was going to another yard with her. I literally crawled along the road until a taxi stopped and brought me home.

That night I received an email from her. She said she couldn't work with me anymore, so she closed all the shops and paid off all the staff.

I decided I could not let that happen. I decided to walk away from the business instead and leave her to it, no matter that it was between £30-50,000 of personal equipment and furniture.

The next day I put the keys through the door of the business and turned my back on everything it was worth. Later I learned she had told the insurance company to pay the money for the floods into her personal account. I walked away with nothing.

I have had no contact with my mother since.

Such a bitter pill to swallow, especially as I'd bought her a wee dog for her birthday. I invested so much time because I had to keep this beautiful wee bundle of wool after my stepfather stated he didn't want another dog, but my mother wanted a mate for the dog she already had.

I agreed to purchase her a puppy and off we went to Johnstone to see some pups. When we arrived, this beautiful little dog climbed onto my knee just as if she knew me, and we fell in love with her and ended up taking her away. She was only eight weeks old and curled up on my knee as we drove home. Within two weeks, this wonderful little ball of life was toilet-trained and knew her name. We had a little bed for her on top of my bed so when she needed attention, I wouldn't find accidents all over the house. She was like your very own alarm clock and at 6.30 am every morning she'd walk up to me and lick the side of my face as if she was telling me 'I want out.' I'd lift her onto the floor, and off she'd go.

Once she came back in, she'd wait for me to lift her up, and she'd go back into her bed for a couple of hours. She was so intelligent and used to love to lay on my chest. Had she been sent to help me, and did I really want to give her up? This went through my head continually, but I remembered I'd bought her as a gift for my mother.

As Millie got bigger, she'd climb into my jacket pocket and later into my backpack so we could cross the road and go to the shop, where she followed me everywhere. It broke my heart when my mother took her home, knowing she was going to be used for continual breeding like a puppy factory and that I'd never see her again.

12. MY CALLING TO WORK IN SPIRIT

I was left with nothing. I had no job, no business, and no marriage. I did not even have my health. I should have been at rock bottom. Now I know that only by clearing away those worldly things was I truly ready to enter my next life phase. And that my brother would be my guide.

It started in August 2008. I was asleep in bed, and suddenly I woke up. A white light appeared, and I heard my brother's voice very clearly. He said, 'Come through the light.'

The following day I felt nothing but relief. I thought I was finally getting out of this life. I thought my brother's words were an instruction, and I was glad. My life had very little love, and it was a very lonely existence.

I decided to end it all. I wrote my notes and said my goodbyes, though I told no one what I was going to do. My intention was to just drop from a motorway bridge. It would be over so quickly, and I would be gone. I would be hit by a vehicle going at seventy miles an hour, and I would be dead. I wouldn't feel a thing.

I can't describe my thoughts as I walked to the bridge. The world and all its treasures meant nothing to me. Soon I would be leaving it all behind. I was almost happy

It didn't quite work like that. A friend found me and brought me home. My mother called my doctor. She wanted me to be sectioned.

However, I was very lucky in my choice of doctor. Or perhaps luck had nothing to do with it. Spirit always finds a way. We had a chat, and I told him about the message. He said he believed what I was told was to come *to* the light, not *through* the light. He asked if I would go and speak to people at Edinburgh College of Parapsychology.

I did that, and they were very interested in me. They decided they would put me in a group that was trying to understand energy.

My ability was forcing itself into the light. I did a card reading for someone who became a friend of mine whose father-in-law was seriously ill. I'll never forget what happened. It was quarter past three in the afternoon when I did the reading. In the end, she asked me a question. 'How long do you think we've got him for?'

I flipped a card. It said eight. I told her, 'Within an eight. You've got him for eight years, eight months or eight weeks, I can't be more specific than that.'

She replied, 'Well, it's not going to be eight months or eight years. It will be eight weeks.'

The following day she called me. He had died at quarter past eleven the previous night – eight hours after the reading. That frightened me. It meant what I had was real.

Then I started to have prophetic dreams, which had never happened before. I started dreaming about helicopter disasters.

In the first dream, I knew that a helicopter crashed and all 18 people on board survived, but in the second dream… in that one, I was helping to lift bodies onto the shore. There were 16 of them.

On February 18, 2009, a Eurocopter EC225LP helicopter ditched in the North Sea. All 18 people on board were rescued.

When I heard the news, I went cold. I could hardly believe it. Then I realised that dream had come true…

On April 1, 2009, Bond Offshore Helicopters Flight 85N crashed into the sea northeast of Peterhead. All 16 people on board were killed.

My ability was getting stronger.

In 2013, I foresaw the Clutha helicopter disaster in which a police helicopter crashed into a packed Glasgow pub – killing all three helicopter occupants and seven people in the pub. I saw the helicopter drop from the sky, but unfortunately, I didn't know where it was going to happen.

The energy class at the College of Parapsychology was a way of getting started because to work with energy, you must start small, for example, sensing the messages on cards. It was about learning to feel your energy and how to stretch it. Feeling and sensing other people's auras, feeling energies from drawings or pictures that people would bring, all that sort of stuff. There was a lot of talking about energy, and after a while, it got boring.

I decided I couldn't do it. Then the principal, Angela, asked me if I would go into a development class. I said I'd give it a go, but I didn't think it was for me. I sat in that class for six months and got absolutely nothing.

AN EARTHBOUND ANGEL

I used to say to the tutor, 'I'm cool, I'm all sorted,' and even though I tried the exercises, I didn't feel I'd done very well. I stayed with it, though, even though I considered leaving several times, but it seemed that Spirit had other ideas, just as my tutor had. Two weeks later, I'd grown so much, and this ability waiting to burst out had fully arrived so my tutor began to take me to churches with her.

The tutor and I were quite close, so she gave me opportunities to work. My part was to deliver the address, which is part of the service, before the medium begins. It gave me a good idea of what went on in the services.

I went on workshops with different mediums, but I wasn't getting anything, really.

My sensitivity, my intuition, was still really strong. That never left. If anything, it was getting stronger. The meditation and the sitting in workshops didn't work for me. I could feel the energy, but I wasn't getting the messages and the proof that everybody else was. It was just weird. I had had enough and was about to give it all up.

Then, in 2011, I went to a workshop with a medium called Val Williams. Val was a member of the Spiritualist National Union, so she was very staunch, very straight and directed.

I agreed to go to the workshop, but I wasn't convinced the outcome would be any different to the previous ones I had attended. I would do this one last workshop, but I had already decided that I wouldn't be going back when we broke for the summer. My attempt to work with Spirit would be over.

But, as I described in Chapter One, Spirit had other ideas, and after breaking through with a message from Diana, I knew I was on the right course.

My tutor began making appointments for me to start taking my own church services. My first service was in Arbroath, and my second was in Kilmarnock. Nobody who had just started their journey got to do the main service in Kilmarnock. That was always done by an experienced medium, but I was put forward to do it.

It was overwhelming. I was so nervous and anxious before each service that I became ill, but I didn't want to disappoint people. Each time I took a deep breath and decided to have a go and see what happened. It was bloody hard. I always had to do my meditation beforehand. But for some reason, it flowed.

And people tell me I made it look easy.

It certainly wasn't easy, but I was becoming able to connect to Spirit without a struggle. It did seem very natural, but I needed my tutor to steer me and guide me to not say too much or not say anything that could offend or upset someone with my message. After a service, you'd go for a Hostess tea with the chairperson or the committee members of the church. You waited to be invited and never insisted on inviting yourself to take a service. I was so busy travelling everywhere, and it might take hours to get there for a service of less than an hour. My tutor sometimes laughed and said, 'Are we mad to do this?'

In June 2012, the Spiritualist National Union awarded me the Conan Doyle Prize. This is awarded to people who are outstanding in the field and who have gone through tough times to get there. That meant I was their organisation's most outstanding new medium that year. They were so impressed with my work they said they would have given me a higher award if they could.

The Conan Doyle Prize was the realisation that all the hard work I'd put in was worth it. I couldn't believe it. I was blown away. For the first time in my life, I felt I belonged.

After that, I began to work in Norway, Denmark, Sweden and Germany.

Who would have thought that all those years of suffering and not knowing the truth would have led me to enlightenment at this point in my life?

The one thing that had always puzzled me was my tutor's insistence on working for anyone other than churches. She used to say that the churches love you one day and drop you the next. Well, that is true, and you do not know how this journey might change your life or the new pathway it might take. As you become more sensitive to Spirit, you must learn to become a little thick-skinned to criticism. This is very hard to do because of your natural sensitivity, but it's essential for coping with the jealous side of spiritualism. Who would have thought that a spiritual circle would not be that spiritually developed? It all depends on how people and behaviours change as you develop your abilities.

I had just turned 40, but it was as if life had just begun. My tutor would tell me that if I hadn't had all those negative experiences in my life, I wouldn't be able to help grieving families. She told me:

'What you are doing now is healing hearts, uniting families and removing grief from their lives so that their thoughts of the past become memories instead of sorrows.

If you can help one person or change the view and understanding of one person, then you've done your job. This is a wonderful ability, but it can become a curse if you are not careful and diligent.

You've been given this wonderful ability, but remember, spirit works with a dirty vessel just as well as they work with a clean vessel. If this gift is abused, it can be taken away or blocked until you finally realise it is there to aid and help people and to understand that spirits are all around us.'

13. REFLECTIONS ON MY LIFE

My grandmother died on Mother's Day in 2012. I had sent her flowers every Mother's Day, but that year I couldn't get them delivered on a Sunday. They could, however, deliver them on a Saturday, and I agreed to that.

She got her flowers on Saturday afternoon, was taken to hospital on Saturday night, and died on Sunday.

I was taking a service in Aberdeen at the time, and I felt it. I felt something wasn't right. After the service, my phone was full of missed calls from my aunt. Not my father, but my aunt, to tell me my gran had passed away.

I was devastated. Six months before she passed, she had started saying to me, 'You know I love you, son, don't you?' It became a regular thing on every call. She said, 'Don't you ever question how much you're loved.'

I wondered why. What was going on that I didn't know about?

On the day of my gran's funeral, her neighbour Francis, who was a medium herself, told me, 'For years, your gran and I would sit on a Wednesday night and connect with your grandad and your brother.'

AN EARTHBOUND ANGEL

Gran never told me.

She used to tell us that her mother could read the tea leaves, so there was obviously ability in the family. It was just never discussed. Even when we were at Granny Brown's, she'd do her party piece and leave you going, 'Wow! How did Granny Brown know that!' it was never spoken about at all. In a strange way, I find it funny and even intriguing. I'm sure she knew all her life that I had the ability, but she never said. She kept reminding me, 'Son, if you need anything, come to me.'

Gran was just so protective of me. I learned she did not like showing her emotions, but she clearly loved me like a son. My great-aunt tells me that the first person Gran loved to talk about was me, yet it so often felt to me that she was ready to push me away.

She is very, very much missed. Very sadly, after her passing, our family fell apart, and it doesn't look like we will reunite. The rifts are too deep.

Relationships and the traumas arising from them do scar children, and they carry those scars into their adult lives. But, from time to time, when I talk about difficulties with my family, my close friends keep reminding me, 'You are part of a much bigger family now. A bigger family that will give you all the love you ever need. It's just not in a physical form.'

And they do. I wouldn't be in the position I am if it was not for the spirit world opening doors for my ability.

I have a lot of self-respect, but I still don't have a lot of confidence. Throughout my journey, I have been dogged by jealousy because of my ability and how naturally it has come. I can't help that, but because I'm so sensitive, it affects me.

My circle is very small because I can't now let people in that I can't trust.

When I think about Caroline, I don't think our marriage would have lasted the test of time, especially now that my spirituality is here and my ability has arrived.

In my heart of hearts, I have known all my life what has been wrong for me, but I have not been brave enough to say, 'Stop!'

That was the case with my marriage, but I couldn't discuss it. I just internalised it, and that made me worse.

I want to help people starting this journey to enlightenment understand that when their life starts to change, it doesn't mean it is changing for the worse. The changes affected me mentally, and I began to question my fundamental self. People who are not strong could end up in a dark place due to the reorientation that necessarily comes about when one is trying to balance the self. Some men and women have started on this journey and ended up taking their own lives because they didn't understand how they would change, and they worried how their lives would be upended and even ruined because their abilities arrived.

When I reflect upon my life, I realise I've experienced most of the things that can happen to a person. That helps me understand where other people are in their lives. Then, when I connect with them, I can provide the right amount of sentiment and the right amount of humour to help heal hearts and unite families, especially those that are grieving.

AN EARTHBOUND ANGEL

Mediums do some phenomenal work. For example, a chap called Lee lived next door to me. When my journey began in 2009, he came to me because he knew I was sitting in a development circle. He said, 'If I give you some coordinates, can you tell me what you see?'

I described a yellow campervan with a white roof. I said Germany was important. I described two vehicles where there was a switch of plates. These were all things that he himself had seen and now that I had confirmed his vision, he was going to take it to the police in connection with the disappearance of Madeleine McCann.

The police turned him away. Years later, what did we see on the news but the exact same campervan, the car and the switch of plates that I had described. It was a yellow camper van with a white roof. The door was open, and Madeleine had left the apartment to look for her mummy.

I remember once, during a healing session, I heard a voice on my left say, 'Hi, I'm Vikki,' and on my other side say, 'I'm Dinah,' and then suddenly at my back was another saying, 'I'm Angelika.' I was in the vestry when these voices went on to tell me how they were abducted and who the perpetrator was, and to watch out for Peter. I didn't fully understand what they meant or what was going on. Once I came back around, I asked the facilitator, but she gave me some excuse about being busy working with other victims. I have since learned that these beautiful souls were trusting me, and I could perhaps have helped them more. Perhaps I could have shared this with the authorities to look for other cases to help make a connection to solve a case. It's not unusual for people with abilities to help; after all, that's how Osama Bin Laden and Saddam Hussain were captured by military forces after a tip-off from a medium. There are some charlatans who make the police doubt it is worthwhile. Our organisations should look more closely at how Sensitives with ability could help to gather information about serious events, then we might solve some crimes sooner rather than later. Instead, we are dismissed completely.

The late Colin Fry campaigned and tried to reach out to Spiritual Organisations to come together and start to register acclaimed and bonafide psychics and mediums. He never saw this wish come to life, but it will have to come one day, I believe. People also need to know that a psychic and a medium are different. The easy way I learned to understand this was that a psychic will read your hopes, wishes and dreams, while mediums deal in facts. All mediums have psychic abilities, but psychics are not mediumistic. You can't be taught how to become a medium because it's got to be born in you. You can, however, have the right conditions created with the right guidance to help you understand how to tap into your abilities.

I'm happy where I am in my life. I'll never stop trying to do my best and striving for the best.

I guess the one thing that keeps me going is the love I have for my brother in the spirit world and my gratitude to him. I shall always be indebted to him for opening this door. I now wish that perhaps things could have been different between us. I hope that writing this book helps the healing process and takes some of the pain away.

AN EARTHBOUND ANGEL

When I was a child, I wanted to be a teacher. Through my spiritual journey, I'm able to teach others in a very different way. And hence, another reason for this book is to educate: to teach others that it is okay to be different and that you have to understand this lesson for yourself before you can share it with anyone else.

The one thing I have learned from my experiences is that Spirit will look after you, and it will make sure you're in the right place at the right time. Spirit can't quite pay your physical bills, but it can move mountains when you need it.

The example I use is when I needed money to take the NHS to court for negligence. There was no way I could raise the sum required, but the barrister told me to apply for Legal Aid. On my late brother's birthday, a letter dropped through the door, telling me that my Legal Aid had been granted. Was that a coincidence?

There is no such thing as coincidence.

My life has been a closed book until now. I am opening up in this book because I feel using my experiences to help others is important.

Although there has been a lot of sadness in my life, along with a lack of love and *a lot* of change, I think all the signs that I should have been working for Spirit have always been there if only I had recognised them. Anyone who has seen me at work has seen a completely different person from the one they see in my everyday life. When the spirit world takes over, it alters your mind because Spirit is coming in through you. When I work for Spirit, I do not feel the pain from my injuries, though I pay for that later.

I would still say that if you gave me the choice to leave this life tomorrow or stay, I would choose to leave. However, I'm at a stage in my life now where I'm happy with myself. I know who I am. Life doesn't frighten me anymore.

Once you commit yourself to the spirit world, it is the most rewarding, humbling feeling you could ever experience. Although a lot of people allow the ego to come in and edge God out, if you can stay solid and keep your feet on the ground, you will forever be rewarded. Always remember to live the way you preach, teach or engage.

I am privileged to do what I do and will be humble for the rest of my life. I understand now that it's not about money. It's about satisfaction in what you do.

And, for me, that is healing hearts and minds and bringing peace.

I now look forward to these up-and-coming changes and understanding the spirit world as my life goes on.

Transformation

As you grow, your abilities grow and change too. These include transfiguration and physical mediumship if you have these in your spiritual arsenal. As we grow, we learn to understand these and how to give up partial or full control of our minds, and as a result, phenomena can happen.

I include some photographic evidence — pictures that were taken whilst I was demonstrating both at a church and under a red light. All of them show distinct changes and show spirit and the healers or just the spirit entity. The sitter or audience can see this for themselves.

This is just a snapshot of how your abilities are limitless. Watch out for more on this coming soon!

Love, light and blessings always.

Graham

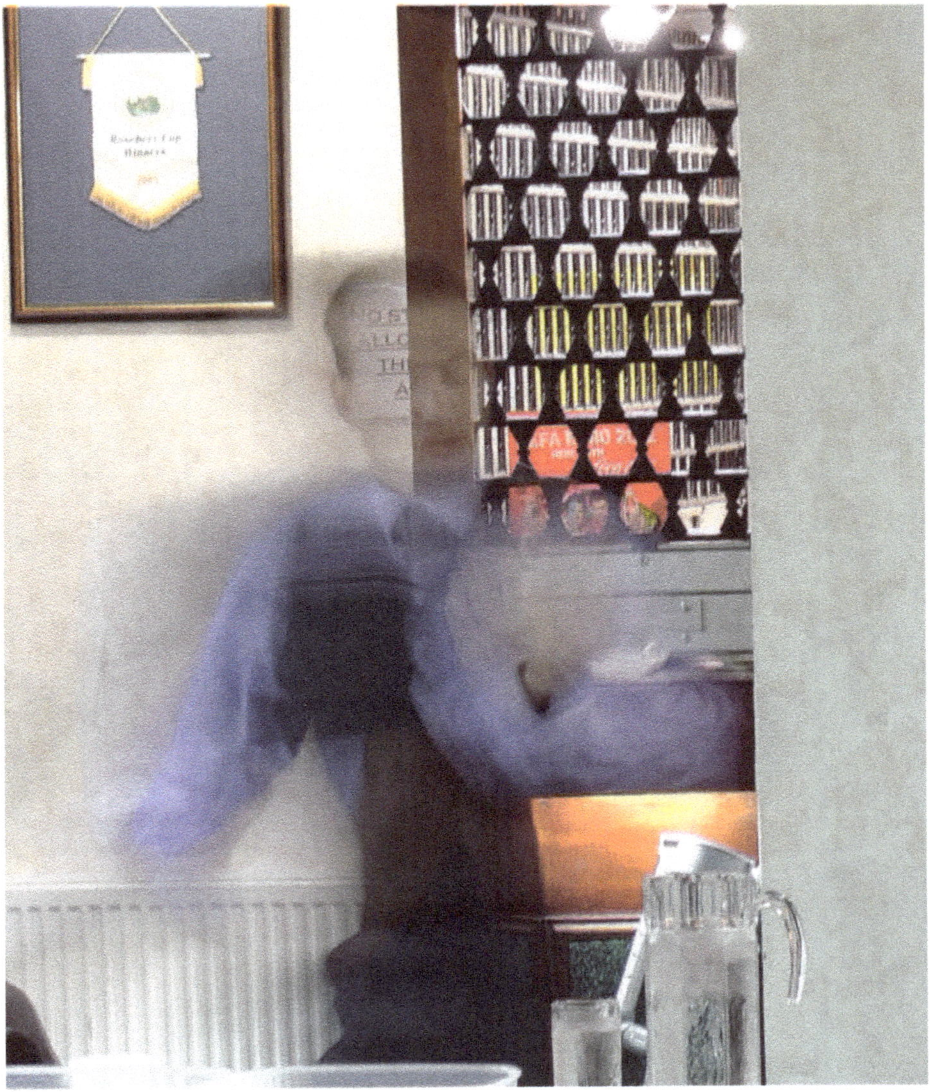

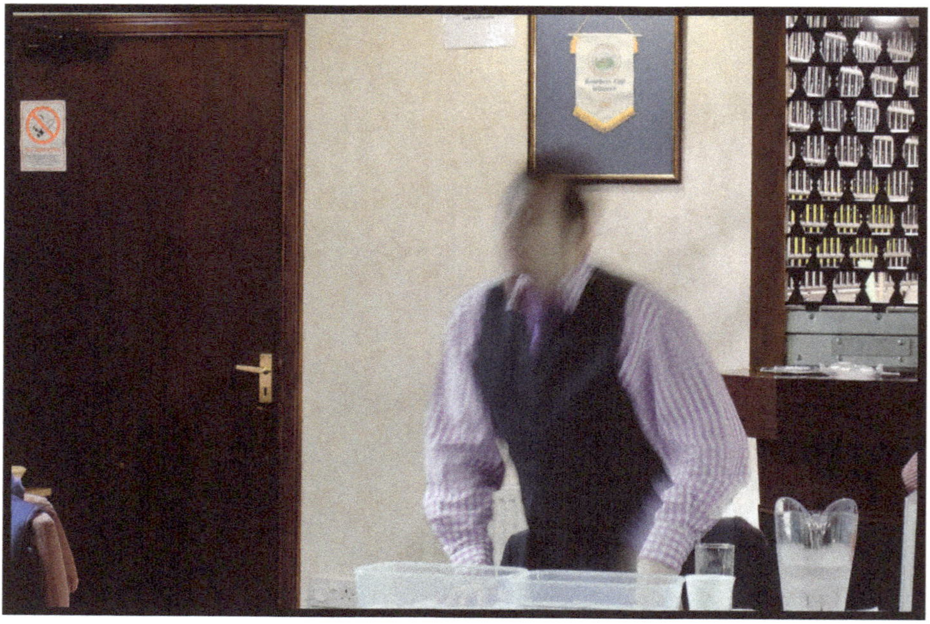

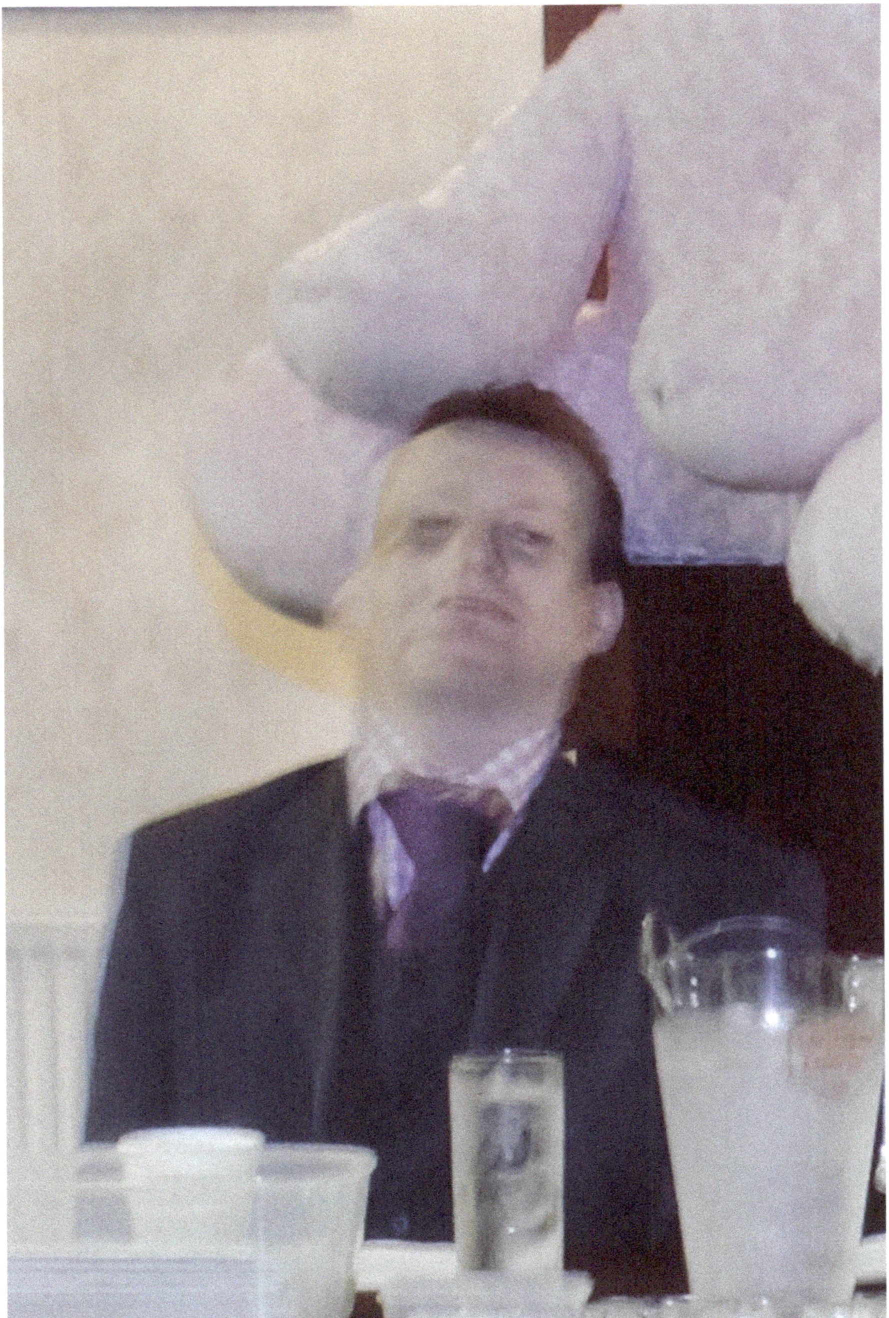

No S...
ALLO...
TH...
A...

Milton Keynes UK
Ingram Content Group UK Ltd.
UKHW020759071223
433901UK00001B/1

9 781739 548629